HITTIN' THE TRAIL: MINNESOTA

Minnesota's Best Autumn Hikes

By Rob Bignell

Atiswinic Press · Ojai, Calif.

MINNESOTA'S BEST AUTUMN HIKES

A GUIDEBOOK IN THE
HITTIN' THE TRAIL: MINNESOTA SERIES

Atiswinic Press
Ojai, Calif. 93023
dayhikingtrails.wordpress.com

ISBN 978-1948872140

Cover design by Rob Bignell
Cover photo of Congdon Park in Duluth, Minn.

Manufactured in the United States of America
First printing August 2021

Dedication

For Kieran
"Like the north wind whistlin' down the sky
I've got a song, I've got a song"
- Jim Croce, "I Got a Name"

Autumn leaves shroud Split Rock Lighthouse.

Contents

Introduction

Autumn in Minnesota is like living in a painting. Before the all-pervasive green of summer gives way to the stark white of winter, fall celebrates with masterful brushstrokes, from the ambers and golds of aspen and birch to the crimson and purples of sumac and white ash, from the brilliant yellows, oranges and red of maples to the scarlet and russets of oaks. Accenting this are the fiery reds of prairie grasses, the bronze cornstalks of farm fields, the oranges of pumpkins and gourds, and the carmines of plump ripe apples and cranberries. When September arrives, nature has found her palette.

There's no better way to explore Minnesota's varied colors than a hike. While fall color road tours are popular, sitting inside a motor vehicle is a bit like watching a movie about pretty autumn leaves. You don't breathe in the crisp, fresh autumn air or feel against your skin the last warm rays of sunlight before winter arrives. You don't hear the crunch of fallen leaves or acorns beneath your feet. You don't find yourself immersed in a canopy of color but instead must focus on open asphalt, as it winds alongside a creek or river stuck in your peripheral vision. You don't stop to enjoy a warm mug of apple cider or a caramel apple pulled from your backpack but instead must keep hands on the wheel.

Fortunately for Minnesota's residents and visitors, great places to hike abound. These trails also offer significantly different experiences, from the harvest-hued rainbows of the Driftless Area's hills to the golden ribbon of riversides, from the vast orange and red forests of the Northwoods to the farm field and woodlot quilt of the state's plains. In **Minnesota's Best Autumn Hikes**, we've listed the top 10 fall foliage trails, as well as offered the best hikes in each of the state's regions and counties. More than 100 fantastic day hikes are listed here, and all are guaranteed to delight.

Why Hike in Autumn?

Though summer has passed, that's no reason to put the hiking boots at the back of the closet until next May. Autumn actually is a great time to hit the trail.

Why? Because there are:

• **Cool, dry days** – As winter approaches, summer's heat and humidity dissipates. Late morning through the early afternoon, however, still can see warm, comfortable temperatures that might require a sweatshirt and jeans rather than T-shirt and shorts.

• **Fewer bugs** – Cool, dry days mean few mosquitoes and virtually no other creepy crawlies, as they prefer standing water and warm air. Most insects' life cycles have reached their end in September.

• **Better sightlines** – As leaves fall to the ground, the landscape opens up, allowing you to spot interesting geological features or terrain that summer's thick foliage keeps hidden.

• **More animal sightings** – Birds migrate while mammals gorge in preparation for winter's cold. As the foliage no longer is as thick, seeing them is easier.

• **No crowds** – Kids are back to school, football fans are camped out in front of the TV, and whoever else is left wrongly thinks last night's frost means the whole day will be cold. That makes for a quiet, peaceful trek on almost any given autumn day.

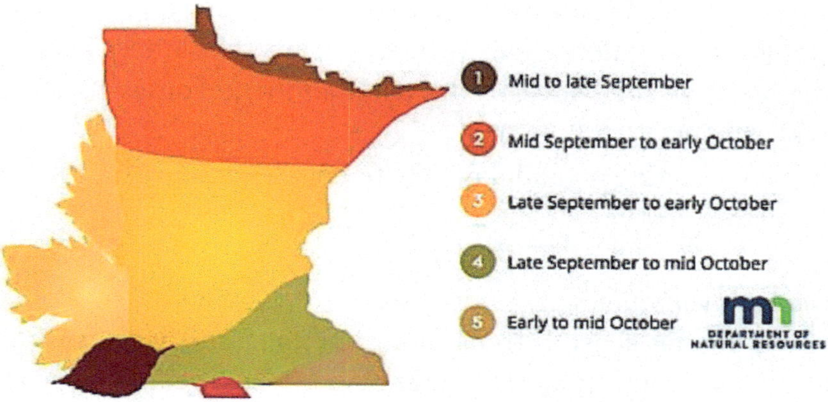

Leaves hit their peak fall colors in northern Minnesota a few weeks earlier than in the state's southern part. Illustration courtesy of Minnesota Department of Natural Resources.

Of course, not all trees change color in autumn. You may recall from elementary school science that there are two types of trees – deciduous and coniferous. Deciduous trees spread their seeds through flowers each spring and sport leaves that change color and fall off each autumn. They include maples, oaks, birch, aspen, poplar, basswood and elm, to name just a few. Coniferous trees use cones to spread their seeds and have needles that don't change color or fall. Among them are pines, cedar and spruce. There is a third kind of tree, though – a deciduous coniferous, which has needles that change color and fall off. In Minnesota, the tamarack is one such tree.

While large swaths of Minnesota are pineries and prairies, deciduous trees still abound. Because of this, every county has at least a couple of hiking spots to enjoy autumn leaves.

Choosing a Trail

Knowing a little about how tree leaves change color can ensure you won't be disappointed on an autumn hike. It'll also mean you can avoid crowds by taking trails that others haven't thought of, as they stick to the tried-and-true routes listed in travel articles.

When selecting a good day hike to enjoy fall foliage, consider four factors.

Streams/river valleys

Early in the season, trees along streams and river valleys will change color first. That's because areas near water are cooler than land at the same altitude that is away from water. Railroad beds converted into trails make for great early autumn hikes as rail lines tended to run along river shores and through wetlands, which in the past were deemed land of little value.

Apple orchards

Apples trees usually only grow on soils that drain well and can take deep roots, so there likely are a greater variety of trees nearby than there would be in low-lying wet areas. Trails passing orchards mean a greater palette of color, and apples hanging from the branches only add more hues.

Lots of vertical gain

Hike from the bottom of a hill to its summit, and you'll pass through a variety of ecosystems, each with its own set of trees that prefer the temperature, soils and amount of sunlight available at specific elevations. Trails leading to observation or fire towers are perfect for gaining altitude, especially at midseason.

North sides

Sometimes trees on the side of a hill facing away from the

sun will produce more brilliant colors than those with a southern face. That's because daytime temperatures on the south side are warm for an extended period, which tends to result in a flatter coloration. Trails that head around the northern base of a hill or bluff before nighttime freezes begin usually offer better autumn colors.

A final note: If spring was wet and the summer temperate, expect good autumn colors.

Leaf Colors

Ever go on an autumn hike and wonder what kind of tree sported such brilliantly colored leaves?

Depending on the tree and where you live, that might not be a problem. Just about every kid in Wisconsin and Vermont can identify a maple tree and tell you when you're looking at an oak. Still, there are plenty of other trees out there that most of us can't name.

You may want to bring along a tree guidebook the next time you hit the trail during autumn. Part of the fun of a fall hike can be identifying the different colored leaves that wash across the horizon like a watercolor painting.

To help make your identification of the tree easier, here's a list of what color various common trees turn each fall.

Yellow

American elm (yellow)
Balsam poplar (yellow)
Big-toothed aspen (yellow)
Black ash (yellow) *4*
Black cherry (yellowish red)
Black walnut (yellow)
Box elder (yellow)

Cottonwood (gold)
Hackberry (yellow)
Honey locust (yellow)
Ironwood (dull yellow)
Locust (buttery yellow)
Paper birch (yellow) *2*
Pin cherry (bright yellow)
Poplar (yellow)
Quaking aspen (amber) *1*
Red mulberry (yellow)
Silver maple (pale yellow)
Yellow birch (yellow)

Orange
Black maple (orange, though also can be yellow or red)
Chestnut oak (brownish orange)
Hickory (gold to orange)
Mountain maple (bright orange, though also can be red)
Oak (orange)
Sugar maple (brilliant orange, yellow and red) *12*

Red
Northern pin oak (bright scarlet)
Northern red oak (bright red) *6*
Red maple (scarlet)
Sumac (deep crimson)

Purple/Burgundy
Cinquefoil (purple)
Dogwood (purple)
Virginia creeper (deep burgundy)
White ash (deep maroon)

Brown
Bur oak (brown, though also can be yellow) *9*
Butternut (brown, though also can be yellow)
Swamp white oak (brown)
White oak (brown, though also can be red)

Green
Basswood (olive) *5*

Evergreens (no leaves)
Balsam fir *10*
Black spruce *7*
Northern white cedar *3*
Red pine *8*
Tamarack (orange needles) *11*

Photo Tips

Sometimes when hiking during autumn, you want to capture the beauty of an area's fall foliage to share with others. Here are some photo tips to consider when out on a fall day hike.

Plan ahead

Know what kinds of trees will be on the trail and if their leaves actually have changed color. Determine how long you have to drive to the trailhead and walk the trail otherwise you might not reach the site you wish to photograph until nightfall. Winging it often will lead to disappointment.

Time your shots

Sunlight comes from the side and is at its warmest at dawn and dusk. Photographs taken early in the morning and late in the afternoon tend to brings out leaf colors.

Keep the sun to your back

If you shoot into the sunlight, glare will wash out the autumn leaf colors. Always take the shot from the angle in which the sun is directly to your back.

Contrast autumn leaves with something blue...

Fall foliage reflecting off a blue lake/river of set against a blue sky will make the leaf colors pop. Using only brown tree trunks to contrast with the leaves will flatten the colors.

...or better yet, contrast with something gray

As saturated colors, autumn leaves will look great against gray, overcast skies. The color from the obscured sun will be soft and diffused so that glare isn't an issue.

Follow rule of thirds

Don't just focus on the leaves. Include some foreground (the ground or waterway before the trees or even the tree trunks) and some background (such as sky). The photo then consists of three parts – the ground/waterway/tree trunks, the colored leaves, and the sky. Just make sure the leaves take up a larger percentage than either of the other two parts alone but not more than the other two parts combined.

Keeping Kids Warm

As the weather cools, summer's T-shirt and shorts rarely are sufficient except during the rare heat wave. Your clothing choices need to change for autumn. Fortunately, ensuring kids stay warm and comfortable during an autumn day hike is easy to do. Just follow these simple guidelines:

- **Layer clothing** – Dressing children in a T-shirt, long-sleeved shirt, and windbreaker actually will keep them warmer and dryer than having them wear a single bulky piece of clothing. Layering offers the added benefit of being able to take off and put back on layers of clothing as the weather warms or cools through the day.

• **Avoid cotton and denim** – Though comfortable, these materials take a long time to dry and so are bad news when children get wet. Opt for synthetics, especially for outer layers.

• **Don wool socks** – Rain boots are great for keeping feet dry, but the rubber does little to keep one's feet warm. The solution is to wear wool socks, which are superior to cotton socks in retaining body heat.

• **Wear a hat** – Brimmed hats are great for keeping the sun and rain drops out of one's eyes. In colder weather, a stocking cap will help keep the body warm by preventing heat loss through the head.

• **Choose mittens over gloves** – The former will keep children's small fingers warmer than the latter. If gloves are a necessity (They do make manipulating objects easier!), be sure to get fleece-lined ones.

Games and Activities

One of the best ways to make a hike memorable – especially for children with you – is to play a few games or activities. You always can go for the tried and true I Spy-styled diversions, but sometimes playing a game or pausing for an activity that is unique to the season is really special. The kids then may be having too much fun to even realize they're also learning something! Here are three fun games and activities I did on hikes with my son when he was younger.

Leaf Crown

Collect a dozen or so leaves along the trail. Only select leaves that are clean and have stems. Don't use those with holes or that are dry and brittle. Maple leaves are particularly ideal.

Fold one leaf in half. Bring a second leaf's stem to the first leaf's top (or the end opposite of the stem). Weave the first stem's leaf into the second leaf.

Fold the second leaf. Bring a third leaf's stem to the second leaf's top. Weave the third stem's leaf into the second leaf.

Keep repeating until you have weaved enough leaves to encircle your child's head. With the last leaf, fold it in half. Bring the stem of the very first leaf used in making the crown to the last leaf's top. Weave the stem into the last leaf.

Place on head.

Talk with your child about how leaves work by using photosynthesis. You may want to read up on the subject before hitting the trail.

Materials: Dozen leaves

Ages: 3 and up

Fall Leaf Suncatchers

During the hike, have each child collect five freshly fallen leaves. The leaves can be different colors or hues of the same color. To prevent leaves from cracking, you may want to place them in a plastic re-sealable bag.

Once home, have the children cut a five- or six-inch diameter hole out of the center of a paper plate. Next, cover the hole by pasting clear wrap to one side of the paper plate. Wax paper will work in a pinch.

Have children arrange the leaves they collected in a pattern on the side of the paper plate that the clear wrap was glued to. Easy tiny drops, children then glue their leaves onto the clear wrap.

Paper punch a hole at the top of the paper plate, about halfway between the plate's edge and the clear wrap. String yarn through the hole and tie.

Hang the paper plate on a curtain rod over a window. The leaves will filter and glow in the sunlight.

Materials: Leaves, paper plates, scissors, clear wrap, glue, paper punch, yarn

Ages: 3 and up

Leaf Line-up

Have each child pick one leaf that they see along the trail. At a rest break, have the kids line up the leaves based on their different qualities: shortest to tallest; thinnest to widest; shortest to tallest stems; least to most leaf points, etc. To make it a competition, score a point for whoever has the tallest, widest, most points, etc.

Materials: Leaves found along trail

Ages: 3 and up

Trail Mix

Have kids help you make homemade trail mix, also known among backpackers as gorp. Here's how to make an autumn mix variety of gorp. You'll need 8 cups of popcorn, 4 cups of pretzels, and 2 cups of candy corn. Mix it in a large bowl or pour into a gallon-size re-sealable zipper bag and shake.

Maps

To properly prepare for any hike, you should examine maps before hitting the trail and bring them with you. No guidebook can reproduce a map as well as the topographical maps or aerial photos you can find online for free. To that end, a companion website (*dayhikingtrails.wordpress.com/trail-maps/#minnesota*) to this book offers printable maps for each listed trail.

Autumn leaves line a backroad on Minnesota's North Shore near Lutsen.

The 10 Best

Minnesota enjoys a rich array of trees and ecosystems, and thanks to that a bounty of different autumn leaf experiences. You can hike hillsides of yellow, orange and red sugar maples, see swaths of golden aspen and birch in river valleys below, or walk through mixed forests with colors ranging from bronze and scarlet to amber and maroon. In this section, we'll look at the state's best trails for discovering these varied autumn colors.

Quaking aspen (top) and paper birch (bottom) are Minnesota's two most common trees.

Lutsen Access Trail

Superior National Forest & Lutsen Scientific and Natural Area

A forest of aspen and birch overlooking Lake Superior awaits near Lutsen.

The Lutsen Access Trail serves primarily as a snowmobile route (Some maps will show it as the Lutsen Access Snowmobile Trail.). The 3.33-mile round trip segment of the trail described here can be hiked spring through fall, though. By midsummer, however, you'll want to wear pants and even long-sleeved shirts, as the undergrowth flourishes.

From Lutsen, take County Hwy. 5 (aka Ski Hill Road) north. In about 1.5 miles, you'll come to a ditch crossing the road; park off the road here (If no parking is available, drive north and park on Moose Mountain Drive.). The trail, which used to be a forest road, heads east into the woods of Superior National Forest, skirting the bluffside with Lake Superior to the southeast while Eagle Mountain rises in the northwest.

Within short order, the trail enters an aspen-birch forest. The nearly pure stands of the two tree types – which are Minnesota's most common – dominate, though balsam fir, the state's 10th most common tree, also can be found.

After a half mile, the trail crosses into the Lutsen Scientific and Natural Area. The Lutsen unit preserves three undisturbed woodland areas: the bluffside's aspen-birch forest in its southern portion; a paper birch-sugar maple forest in its central section; and a predominantly sugar maple forest across the rest.

The NF-1230 Ski Trail intersects the trail within the SNA. Continue heading straight/east.

The quaking aspen's flat, spade-like leaves flap at the slightest breeze. In autumn when the leaves turn amber, that makes for quite a show, especially so on trees that grow at least six stories tall and under ideal conditions can reach 10 stories.

A pioneer species, aspen quickly replaced northern Minnesota's great pineries and the continent's many forests when they were logged off in the 1800s. Prevention of forest fires has allowed the tree to maintain its hold.

About 800 feet from the NF-1230 Ski Trail intersection, the trail re-enters Superior National Forest. It curves northeast and in about 1600 feet comes back into the SNA.

Preferring limestone-derived soils, aspen and birch thrive on the bluffside, whose bedrock layers once formed the bottom of an ancient tropical sea. The moist but well-drained soils, typical of the North Shore blufflines, is an added bonus for the trees.

Aspen and birch account for a full 40 percent of Minnesota's timberlands. Quaking aspen is the most common of the state's trees, with its quantity more than double of any other species. Paper birch is the state's second most common tree.

Paper birch doesn't much like shade, so it must grow fast to outcompete other trees for canopy space. It typically rises 66 feet high, but some have reached double that height. The sugar maple still beats it out, though, usually growing between 80-115 feet high, so birch often is found in wetter soil, which trees like sugar maple and basswood don't like.

Native Americans used the paper-like bark to make everything from canoes and wigwams to baskets and cups. Today, the birch still is useful in making a variety of products, whether it be spools and toothpicks, snowshoe frames or flooring, paper pulp or interior finish.

In about 3200 feet, the trail reaches an intermittent stream crossing. This marks a good spot to turn back, though the trail does continue northeast into the Superior National Forest.

An upland cedar grove offers a variety of colors at Lutsen SNA. Photo courtesy of Minnesota DNR.

Final note: Scientific and natural areas typically don't have amenities as state parks do, and Lutsen is no exception.

Oberg and LeVeaux Mountain Trails

Superior National Forest

Day hikers can choose between trails that lead to the summit of two prominent tree-covered hills in Superior National Forest's Sawtooth Mountains. The hikes offer fantastic views of autumn scenery.

Both the Oberg and the LeVeaux mountains trails are well-worn paths and spurs off the Superior Hiking Trail. Though technically hills, locals label them as mountains, and for relatively flat Minnesota, they do indeed feel more the latter rather than the former.

To reach the trails, from Lutsen take Minn. Hwy 61 south. Turn right/north onto the unpaved Onion River Road (aka Forest Road 336). After passing between the two mountains, turn into the parking lot for the Superior Hiking Trail on the road's left/west side.

From there, hikers have two options: Oberg Mountain or LeVeaux Mountain.

Oberg Mountain Trail

Fantastic vistas await day hikers on the trail to the summit of the slightly higher of these two mountains. The Oberg Mountain Trail runs 2.25-miles round-trip through the woods.

From the parking lot, follow the Superior Hiking Trail east across Onion River Road. In 0.15 miles, the trail splits; go right/south onto the stem trail.

Most of the uphill portion of the trail comes next on the switchback stem that leads to a loop near the mountain top. Along the stem, the trail gains about 220 feet elevation.

Sugar maple forest in autumn from Oberg Mountain. Oberg Lake sits below the mountaintop.

Upon leveling out, the stem joins the loop on the mountain's western side. Go right/south.

The loop offers nine overlooks, each lit in autumn colors. Among the views is the Onion River and LeVeaux Mountain to the southwest. Stretching southeast-northeast of the mountain is Lake Superior. Rollins Creek runs from the base of the mountain's north side to the southeast into Lake Superior. Moose Mountain rises to the northeast. Oberg Lake, which sports beavers, is on the north side below the mountain.

Maples and pines dominate the mountain, making for a crescendo of colors. The sugar maple is among the few plants whose leaves turn different colors from tree to tree, so there will be streaks of yellow, orange and red, punctuated by the greens of pines and lighter yellow leaves and silver bark of birch trees.

Sugar maples contain three different pigments in their leaves. Each autumn when trees stop making food from chlorophyll, the leaves' greenness disappears, and those pigments

The sugar maple leaf can appear a variety of colors in autumn.

stand out. Which pigment appears depends on how much sunlight the tree receives and genetics.

If a sugar maple is in the shade, it'll turn yellow. If it's in the full sun, expect red. The proportion of sun of shade, as well as the leaves' DNA, affects how they change throughout the day from yellow to red to orange. Usually the top of the tree and its sides turn red first with the inlaid portion of the tree yellow.

Though the sugar maple is the most common tree in neighboring Wisconsin, it's only the 12th most in Minnesota.

On the mountain's north side, the trail climbs about a hundred feet to its summit at 1555 feet elevation. It then gradually descends as coming back to the stem trail. From there, retrace your steps back to the parking lot.

LeVeaux Mountain Trail

A lookout tower awaits day hikers at the top of the LeVeaux Mountain Trail. The longer of the two trails, it runs 3.5-miles round-trip. The trailhead sits on the parking area's west end by following the Superior Hiking Trail into the forest.

The first leg offers an opportunity to see white-tailed deer and even moose. To spot them, though, you'll need to hike at either dawn or dusk when they feed.

Along the way, you'll pass a stem trail for the Onion River Camp and cross that waterway. After a mile, the trail reaches the loop on the mountain's northwest side. Go right/southeast.

In another 0.15 miles, the trail splits once more. Stay on the loop by going left/southwest. From there, the trail turns steep for about 0.2 miles as it gains 150 feet elevation.

The prize for the hard work is the mountain's summit, 1550 feet above sea level, upon which sits a lookout tower. The tower, referred to on some maps and documents as "US Forest Service Fire Lookout Tower, Onion," dates to 1928.

South of the tower is a lollipop trail that circles the top of the mountain's southwest side. It's about 0.3-miles round trip and worth the walk for the views.

Where that lollipop's stem reaches the main loop atop LeVeaux, take the trail south then northeast as it circles the mountain's small top. Among the sights are LeVeaux Creek to the west, as it runs to the southwest and joins Lake Superior. The lake itself stretches from south of the mountain to the northeast. The Onion River heads from the valley north of the mountain to east then southeast of it. Oberg Mountain is to the northeast.

Middle-West Manitou-Misquah-Yellow Birch Loop

George H. Crosby Manitou State Park

Day hikers can walk through a 400-year-old forest of yellow birch on a scenic loop at George H. Crosby Manitou State Park.

The 3.3-mile Middle-West Manitou-Misquah-Yellow Birch Loop combines four trails, as it winds through the highlands overlooking Lake Superior. Along the loop, day hikers can experience a river rumbling over ancient rock and the old growth forest boasting the centuries-old trees.

George H. Crosby Manitou State Park is perfect for hikers and campers who prefer a primitive nature setting. The park has no developed facilities, in accordance with the wishes of its namesake, a famous Minnesota mining executive who was an avid outdoorsman.

To reach the park, from Silver Bay travel north on Minn. Hwy. 61, turning left/northwest onto Minn. Hwy 1. In Finland, go right/northeast onto County Road 7 (aka Cramer Road). Take a right/east into the park, using the lot where the road loops back on itself.

Superior Hiking Trail

The first leg of the loop, the Middle Trail, starts on the lot's north side. This portion of the trail also is part of the Superior Hiking Trail.

In keeping with the park's primitive nature, the gently rolling dirt trail is narrow and crosses several small stones and tree roots. A boardwalk runs over a wet, boggy area, then the trail climbs a rocky slope.

After 0.3 miles, a side trail heads to an overlook. The view is

Yellow birch's trunks are a bronze color, a delightful sight among the autumn leaves.

worth the few extra steps. Past the overlook, the side trail re-joins the main route; at that junction, go right/north onto the Middle Trail.

Among the interesting sights following the overlook is a birch tree growing atop a boulder with roots clinging to the rock as breaking into the ground. The trail next passes an open log shelter that is a great spot for a break.

At 0.9 miles, the Middle reaches the West Manitou River Trail. Go left/northwest onto the latter.

An overlook is 0.15 miles from the intersection. The rock knoll offers a great view of the river valley below. The vista is stunning in autumn, when the changing leaves paint the forest in a rainbow of harvest colors. From there, descend several wooden steps to the Manitou River's cascades.

After taking in the rapids, turn back, following the trail southwest along the river, which can be seen through several tree breaks. The Manitou River rushes over basalt set down in lava flows some 1.1 billion years ago. The water is the color of frothy root beer due to the dead leaves, grasses and other organic material that drain into the waterway; the hard rocky river bottom causes the water to tumble and aerate.

In 0.6 miles, after passing several spurs to campsites, the Superior Hiking Trail splits to the left/north where it crosses the river. Instead, go right/south onto the Misquah Trail and away from the Manitou. This section of the loop heads through an old growth forest for a half-mile with a couple of overlooks just off the trail.

After passing a spur to campground site 7, the trail curves west. In 0.4 miles from the spur, you'll reach the Yellow Birch and Cedar Ridge trails. Go right/northwest onto Yellow Birch.

This portion of the loop also runs through an old growth forest. Some of the birch trees here started as saplings when the Pilgrims first arrived in America. Because of the thick forest, the trail is rugged. Fortunately, in forest conditions, yellow birch trunks typically are tall and clear of limbs at their lower levels. Yellow birch reaches a height of 75 feet with a diameter of up to three feet. It's easy to spot, as its bark, which ranges from shiny yellow to gray-silver, curls into strips. During autumn, its leaves turn bright yellow and gold.

Wildlife frequently can be spotted along this part of the loop. Be forewarned that black bears are among the park's denizens; should you see a bear, simply make loud noises to scare it off. Being noisy while you hike usually is sufficient to keep bears deep in the woods and away from you.

At 0.3 miles, the trail passes a connector to Bensen Lake. Stay on the main route. Then, in another 0.3 miles, you'll reach the road to your parking lot. Follow it right/north to your vehicle.

Skibo Vista Overlook

Superior National Forest

Sweeping, 30-mile views of autumn colors await at the Skibo Vista Overlook.

Located on the Iron Range, the overlook is an easy stroll, consisting of a mere 250 feet of sidewalk. It sits along the 78-mile Superior National Forest Scenic Byway, which connects the Iron Range to the North Shore.

To reach the overlook, from Hoyt Lakes take County Road 15 (aka Skibo Outlook Road, Forest Route 110, and Forest Route 128) south. After passing County Road 129, the lookout is on the left/east.

Located 20 stories above the terrain below, the overlook sits on the Laurentian Divide. One of the continent's great watershed divides, water on the north side of the Laurentian makes its way toward Hudson Bay while that to the south heads either to the Gulf of Mexico or the Atlantic Ocean. The divide stretches from Triple Divide Peak in northwestern Montana, cuts through Minnesota's Iron Range, and ends on the Labrador Peninsula at the 60th parallel.

Surrounding the overlook are the Toimi Drumlins. Formed during the last ice age, viewed from above the drumlin field looks somewhat like a basket of eggs. Drumlins are a series of elongated, teardropped-shaped hills. Around Skibo Vista, each drumlin ridge is about a mile long, a quarter-mile wide, and 30-50 feet high.

Geologists debate exactly how the drumlins formed, but all agree that they were shaped by the glacier's direction – the ridge's tapered end points the way the glacier was flowing. Here the drumlins run in a southwest-northeast direction.

Quaking aspen dominates the drumlins' tops. Their flat

leaves easily flutter in the wind, in autumn giving the appearance of moving yellow seas below the overlook. Surrounding them is evergreen balsam fir.

In the distance to the west and southwest are tamarack lowlands. Tamarack is among 20 species of trees in the world that are "deciduous conifers," meaning they grow cones and sprout needles like conifers but each autumn their needles change colors and fall, just as deciduous trees lose their leaves. Each September, the tall tamaracks – they usually grow between 33-66 feet high with a trunk two feet in diameter – turn a brilliant gold. It is the 11th most common tree in Minnesota and covers about 5 percent of the state's timberlands.

Mixed amid the aspens and tamaracks are pockets of hardwood forests. Sugar maple, basswood, American elm, and oak populate these enclaves, offering hues of orange, red, yellow and brown.

Neighboring Wisconsin's official state tree, sugar maples thrive in the Midwest's and New England's colder climates. It needs a hard freeze to enter winter dormancy, and seed germination only occurs when the thermometer registers just above freezing. Sugar maples rarely are found any further south than Tennessee, and even there the temperature isn't cold enough to produce the sap used to make maple syrup.

Global warming is pushing the sugar maple's range north. It's disappearing from its southern edges while starting to appear in Minnesota's Northwoods. Acid rain and the ensuing soil acidification also has led to the maple's decline in some areas. Meanwhile, the logging off of woodlands allows other tree species to take hold, limiting the maple's ability to expand. The tree doesn't do as well in urban areas either, where the Norway maple is displacing it.

Basswood, whose leaves turn olive in fall, usually are mixed

Tamarack needles turn orange in autumn.

in the canopy with sugar maple.

The tree likes the same rich soils as sugar maples so often are found together in Minnesota forests. Also known as the American linden, the tree grows across the upper Midwest through New England as well as southern Ontario and Quebec. It's easy to spot; the domed crown consists of spreading branches, the bark ranges from gray to light brown with narrow fissures, and the 4-6 inch long heart-shaped leaves alternate with the larger ones on the side nearest the branch. It's Minnesota's fifth most common tree.

A rare find in most forests these days is the American elm, which was almost wiped out when Dutch elm disease spread through its populations during the early 20th century. The tree is large – usually 50 to 70 feet high with a diameter of 24-48 inches. Its wide-spreading branches droop at the ends, making for a showy display of yellow leaves in autumn. Though somewhat shade tolerant and fast growing to outpace other tall tree species, the elm is common on rich bottomlands, and in Minnesota that usually means the southern portion of the state.

On a clear fall day, the Skibo Vista offers quite a view, with multiple Iron Range towns nestled amid the harvest colors. Soaring eagles and migrating hawks often can be spotted overhead.

Not surprisingly, an observation tower for the Superior National Forest used to stand at the overlook, as it's a perfect spot to watch for forest fires. A concrete foundation is all that remains.

The view didn't look like this during Minnesota's early days as a state. When this was Native American land, the area was much more like the boreal forests to the north. Red and white pine dominated, with aspen, paper birch, spruce, and balsam fir finding niches. After the pine was cut, aspen and paper birch took over.

More change likely is to come in the decades ahead, as global warming allows the climatic change pockets to gain a foothold and spread.

DeSoto Trail

Itasca State Park

Day hikers can head into the heart of the backcountry on the DeSoto Trail at Itasca State Park.

While most visitors to the state park stop at the famous headwaters of the Mississippi River, the DeSoto takes hikers into wilderness. The trail runs 5.8-miles round trip. It also is part of the North Country National Scenic Trail.

To reach the trailhead, from Park Rapids take U.S. Hwy. 71 north. Turn left/north onto Minn. Hwy. 200 then south onto County Road 122, using the park's North Entrance. Go right/west on County Road 117. The road becomes Wilderness Drive. Follow Wilderness Drive south and then east through the park; the road eventually becomes a narrow albeit scenic one-way. After passing Elk Lake, watch for a small parking area on the road's left/north side. The trail heads south from the road's right side.

Heavily wooded, the trail begins by passing a small, unnamed pond. The next couple of miles or so, it skirts wetlands at the edge of Clarke and McKay lakes to the east. Between the two lakes, heading east from the DeSoto, is the Crossover Trail, which connects to the Deer Park Trail.

A variety of trees grow along the trail, including oak, maple, paper birch, and red and white pine. Because of this mix, autumn marks a good time to hike it. The wetland areas also will be drier and the bug population down.

Northern red oaks, which prefer to grow in glacial drift and well-drained soils along streams, thrive here. The tree is easy to differentiate from other oaks; its stout branches grow at right angles to its stem branch, resulting in a narrow, round head. Red oaks live up to 400 years.

Northern red oaks, which can soar nine stories high in forests, produce striking, bright red leaves in autumn.

The sixth most common tree in Minnesota, the red oak is enormous. Growing quite straight and quite tall, the red oak can reach up to 92 feet high with a trunk diameter of 39 inches. In old growth forests, the red oak soars even taller, and some even have been measured at 141 feet high. Red oaks grown in open areas, such as lawns, tend to be stouter, though, but can have a trunk diameter of up to 6.6 feet.

A XXL tree like the red oak also produces big acorns, measuring 1-1/8 inches long. With acorns that size, the tree is fairly easy to spot in autumn. The thoroughly fissured bark on mature red oaks is another giveaway. Their leaves turn brilliant red during fall.

The route turns hilly as passing between Radisson Lake to the west and McKay Lake to the east. The intermittent Ga-Gwa-Dash Creek runs to the trail's west but really isn't visible along the walk.

As coming upon the wetlands close to the Picard Lakes, the trail nears its end, which is the junction with Eagle Scout Trail at the head of a pond bordering Hernando DeSoto Lake. Upon reaching the trail junction, retrace your steps back to the parking lot.

Cow Lake Trail

Maplewood State Park

Day hikers can enjoy the bright splendor of sumac and a maple forest during an autumn hike in east-central Minnesota.

The 4.6-mile unnamed lollipop trail – called here the Cow Lake Trail for the major waterbody it circles – sits in Maplewood State Park. The route is a combination of mowed grass and a wide dirt path. Leashed dogs are allowed.

To reach the trail, from Pelican Rapids take U.S. Hwy. 59 north. Turn right/east on Minn. Hwy. 108. The park entrance is in 7 miles. When the entry road, splits go left/south. Just after the RV sanitation station, turn left/east. Follow the road toward Knoll Campground. At the turnaround for drinking water, park on the road's side, and walk east uphill. The trailhead is in about 100 feet on the right/south.

The mowed grass trail heads uphill into an oak savannah with deep crimson sumac alongside the path. At 0.2 miles, the trail enters the woods.

Woodland edges are an ideal place for the smooth sumac. Though actually a shrub rather than a tree, its brilliant red to burgundy leaves make it a popular autumn sight.

Sumac grows up to 18 feet tall. Its leaves often stretch 14 inches long with up to 23 leaflets on a stem.

You're likely to see a lot of sumac bunched together. It can expand quickly by forming a colony as clones sprout from its roots. It also isn't picky about where it lives, liking both part shade and sun, both dry soils and those with average moisture, and both woodland edges and prairies, as well as roadsides and shorelines.

The park sits in a boundary zone between the hardwood forest of the east and the great prairie of the west. Located near the Red River Valley, the Alexandria Moraine runs through the park, dotting it with kames and kettles.

Kames – large piles of sand and gravel deposited by melting glaciers during the last ice age – can rise up to 1500 feet here. In contrast, kettles formed when blocks of ice broke off from retreating glaciers and their weight depressed the surface; as the ice melted, the basin filled with water, forming a lake.

At 0.3 miles, the trail leaves the woods. Bass Lake is on the left/east. Any children hiking with you will be delighted to find that the trail here includes walking across a beaver dam.

After the dam, the trail re-enters the woods. Sugar maple, basswood, American elm, and oak – known as a mesic forest – dominates. Ironwood, aspen, tamarack, and red cedar also can be found in the park and along the trail.

If visiting in spring or summer, the forest floor is a wonderful spot to look for wildflowers. Trillium, bloodroot and liverwort all thrive here. Scattered among the colorful blooms are boulders carried and left by glaciers during the last ice age.

The trail soon joins an old dirt road and crosses a series of small hills. At 1.1 miles, it reaches a four-way intersection; the crossing trail is for horses. Continue straight/south and head on to the loop.

You'll be able to spot Cow Lake through the trees at about 1.4 miles. The hills turn steeper as entering a paper birch and maple woods.

At 1.7 miles, the trail enters a small grass and thistle meadow. The exposure to the sun is short-lived, though, as in a tenth-mile the trail re-enters the woods.

You're now on the bottom side of the loop. A small kettle pond on the right is visible through the trees, as you head downhill through large quaking aspen and elm.

Back on the trail, look for a beaver sign at 2.1 miles and as

During autumn, leaves of the sumac shrub turn a deep red or crimson, making for colorful displays.

coming to the loop's east side, a small kettle pond on the right at 2.4 miles.

A tenth of the mile from the pond, a path diverges right/northeast. This is part of the equestrian trail crossed earlier. Stay on the main trail by going straight/north. The hiking trail is shared with horse riders from there to the four-way intersection where the loop began.

At 2.8 miles, you'll reach an open meadow on the loop's north side. Cow Lake is on the trail's left in the distance to the west, and Beer Lake is on the right/north.

A variety of common prairie wildflowers grow in the meadow. Among them are beardtongue, prairie rose, showy milkweed, and wild onion.

The trail runs along Beer Lake's southern shore at 2.9 miles then leaves the waterbody behind 0.4 miles later and re-enters the woods with its brilliant autumn leaves.

Next up are two spurs, neither of which leads to anything not already seen on the trail.

At 3.5 miles, you'll reach the four-way intersection where the loop began. Go right/north on the stem trail, and retrace your steps past Bass Lake back to your vehicle.

Black Ash Trail

Belle Prairie County Park

Day hikers can walk through a black ash forest at Belle Prairie County Park near Little Falls. But go quick – though Minnesota's fourth most common tree, the black ash faces a very real threat from an invasive species that could wipe it out.

The roughly 1.25-mile Black Ash Trail (the trail actually is unnamed but called that here for convenience sake) cuts through and circles a black ash forest at the park. Along the way, you'll also cross an oak savanna and head alongside a stand of red pine (Minnesota's eighth most common tree), making for a great autumn hike.

To reach the trailhead, from Little Falls take County Road 76/Haven Road north. Turn left/east onto County Park Road and enter Belle Prairie. At the first road junction, park off the side of the main road. Walk the paved road that splits to the right/west. A jeep trail appears on the right/north; that's the trailhead.

The trail curves through an oak savanna, though the tree cover is thicker here than in what typically is thought of as a grassy plain. That's because the savanna is evolving toward a forest.

In about a quarter mile, a side trail branches to the right/north. Continue left-straight/west.

At the next junction, go right/north then left/west. You'll enter the black ash forest, which circles a lowland that experiences seasonal flooding.

Black ash's oblong leaves grow in sets of up to 11 on a long stem. During autumn, the leaves turn a yellow-green with patches of dark red to brown hues.

The tree itself grows between 35 to 75 feet high with trunk

Though a common tree in Minnesota, black ash may soon disappear, as the emerald ash borer threatens to wipe it out.

diameters of 12 to 24 inches. Thick, cork-like gray bark covers the trunk.

Black ash prefers swampy areas in cold climates. Its range stretches from western Newfoundland to southeastern Manitoba, and south across the Midwest from Illinois to northern Virginia. Historically common in its range, more than a billion black ash trees grow just in Minnesota.

Its days may be numbered, though. The emerald ash borer reached Minnesota in the mid 2010s after ravaging the tree's cousins – green and white ash – across much of the northeastern United States.

The exotic metallic green beetle's larvae feeds on the tree's inner bark, disrupting the plant's ability to transport water and nutrients, resulting in death.

The beetle likely arrived in North America via solid wood packing material imported from Asia. It was first found near Detroit in 2002.

At 0.38 miles, the trail junctions a loop heading through a red pine stand. You can skirt the stand and the black ash grove by going left/southwest.

No other large, native trees fill the same role as black ash in its range. If it disappears, large swaths of Minnesota forests could become brushlands of tag alder and invasive buckthorn. That in turn could affect the water table in those lowlands, as black ash pulls out far more moisture from the ground than scrubby brush does.

Views of the Mississippi River appear following the next trail junction at about 0.54 miles. The river is fairly narrow here compared to what you'll find downstream just south of the Twin Cities.

At the next three trail junctions, veer left/east. This takes you along the south side of the black ash forest. To the south, you're certain to see tall white pines rising from the woods; the pines there are nearly 200 years old.

Upon reaching the next trail junction, you're at the east end of the loop circling the black ash forest. Go right-straight/ northeast at the next two trail intersections. You'll then arrive at the single-lane road you walked in on.

The trail through the black ash forest often is muddy, so always wear hiking books and try to hike no sooner than a couple of days after a rainfall.

You'll also want to carry insect repellent, though in fall the chance of bugs bothering you is low.

Bur Oak Trail

Helen Allison Savanna Scientific and Natural Area

Minnesotans can walk one of the state's best remaining oak savannas – a rapidly disappearing ecosystem – at the northern edge of the Twin Cities.

Each autumn, the Helen Allison Savanna Scientific and Natural Area brightens the landscape in harvest hues, as the bur oak's brown and the pin oak's dark scarlet leaves rise above the golden grass. While no maintained trails run through the savanna, game trails and degraded footpaths can be used for a 0.8-mile round trip hike (named the Bur Oak Trail here for convenience sake).

To reach the trailhead, from Minn. Hwy. 65 east of Bethel, take 237th Avenue east. Turn right/south on Gopher Drive, which becomes 229th Avenue. Go right/south on Durant Street; the junction of 229th and Durant marks the natural area's northeast corner. In a little more than 1000 feet, park off the side of the road and head west into the natural area.

When Euro-Americans arrived some two centuries ago, oak savanna once covered around 8700 square miles of Minnesota, stretching in a band from north of what is now the Twin Cities to the Iowa border. Today, just 1 percent of that savanna remains.

A transition area between prairie and woods, the savanna attracts a lot of wildlife, including white-tailed deer and turkey, which feed on the plentiful number of acorns that drop from the trees. You're also certain to hear the red-headed woodpecker pecking for bugs in the oaks' trunks.

The dominant tree in the savanna is the bur oak. It can grow quite tall – up to 98 feet – but many Minnesota savannas have far younger and hence shorter trees. The oaks' trunks also are

Bur oak can be found across Minnesota.

massive, reaching up to 10 feet in diameter.

Not surprisingly, a big tree like the bur oak produces big acorns – in fact the bur oak bears the largest of all North American acorns. Some of them reach up to 2 inches in length and

Northern pin oak primarily grows in eastern Minnesota.

1.5 inches wide.

If conditions are right, the bur oak's leaves will turn yellow in autumn. Older bur oaks often boast gnarly branches, making it a perfect Halloween tree.

The bur oak is Minnesota's ninth most common tree. Though king of the oak savanna, it can be found in every county of the Gopher State.

Northern pin oak also is prevalent in the savanna. Though considered a medium-sized tree and usually shorter than the bur oak, it has been known to achieve some impressive height and girth. The record pin oak in Minnesota rose 95 feet tall with a diameter of 4.5 feet before toppling in a wind storm.

While usually paling in size to the bur oak, the pin oak more than makes up for it with its autumn leaves. They typically turn either a deep maroon or a rusty red. As winter arrives, the color diminishes to brown.

Pin oak is less common in Minnesota than the bur oak. You won't find it in most western prairie counties or the northern aspen-oak forests.

While many of Minnesota's oak savannas have been plowed under into farm fields or paved over into urban areas, the suppression of fire also has contributed to the ecosystem's demise. Without natural fires, shrubs – especially the invasive buckthorn – take over the grasslands. Bur oaks can survive fires, as those older than 12 years are flame-resistant thanks to their thick bark.

As trails are not maintained in the natural area, you'll want to wear pants, long-sleeve shirt, and hiking boots while traversing it. During autumn, a hike following the first nighttime freeze usually means tall grass will be easier to navigate past.

The oak savanna continues north of the natural area at the University of Minnesota's Cedar Creek Ecosystem Science Reserve. While the trails there are in much better shape than those at Helen Allison, stick to the latter. Scientific research is underway at Cedar Creek, so casual visitors aren't allowed.

White Oak Trail

Nerstrand Big Woods State Park

Hikers can walk through a large stand of white oak in Minnesota's famed Big Woods at Nerstrand Big Woods State Park.

The 2.4-mile round trip White Oak Trail runs through the park's center.

To reach the trailhead, from Faribault take County Road 20/ Cannon City Boulevard northeast. Turn right/east onto County Road 30 then right-straight/east onto County Road 88. When the road splits, continue left-straight/east. Go left/north into Nerstrand Big Woods and park at the lot for the picnic area.

The trail heads south from the parking lot. As approaching the county road, the trail veers west and enters the Big Woods.

Nerstrand Big Woods preserves 1280 acres of a forest that is now virtually gone. When pioneers arrived in the area during the mid 1800s, the Big Woods covered 5000 square miles across Wisconsin and Minnesota.

A temperate hardwood forest, American elm, basswood, sugar maple, and red oak dominate the Big Woods' canopy while ironwood, green ash, and aspen ruled the understory. Laura Ingalls Wilder wrote of growing up amid the forest in her novel "Little House in the Big Woods," which takes place at nearby Pepin, Wis.

All of the traditional Big Woods trees can be seen along the trail as it crosses Hickory Bridge. At the next trail junction, go right/north for a surprise: A large stand of white oak thrives along a stretch of the trail.

White oak's name comes from the color of its wood; its bark actually is a light gray. It usually grows up to 50-80 feet high with a massive canopy supported by large branches.

White oaks primarily grow in southeastern Minnesota and

White oak leaves turn bright to wine red in autumn. The tree is found in the Driftless Area and the Twin Cities.

the Twin Cities. It would be a rare find indeed in the Northwoods or western prairie.

During autumn, their leaves turn a bright red to wine red color. Mature oaks drop massive amounts of acorns, so don't be surprised to see squirrels and chipmunks scampering beneath them. Each light brown, oval nut has a semicircular cup atop it.

The tree is extremely long-lived, lasting for around 200-300 years. One white oak in New Jersey was known to be more than 600 years old before dying. White oak is widely used in a number of commercial products because the wood is tough and water resistant. It can be found in boats, cabinetry, flooring, furniture, and wine barrels.

Ignore the next two trails, which come in from the left/west. The trail is a spur that heads to a campsite.

Next, Oak Bridge crosses Prairie Creek, carved out from glacial meltwater at the end of the last ice age some 10,000 years ago. The scenic bridge offers a good view of the tree canopy in the ravine below.

After the bridge, the trail junctions with Beaver Trail at 1.2 miles. This marks a good spot to turn back, though if you're up for it, there are plenty of more oaks on the ascent for the next 0.6 miles.

Minneopa Falls Trail

Minneopa State Park

Day hikers can walk to the most scenic waterfall in southern Minnesota, a perfect adventure in autumn when the gorge glows in orange and red leaves.

The 0.4-mile round trip Minneopa Falls Trail sits in Minneopa State Park near Mankato. The trail is located in the park's smaller southern part.

To reach the trailhead, from Mankato drive U.S. Hwy 169 west. Turn right/north onto County Road 69/Gadwall Road. After entering the park, take the first left/south. The road ends in a gravel parking lot; leave your vehicle there.

Follow the paved path from the parking lot past the picnic area. You'll hear the rush of the falls as you approach Minneopa Creek.

The trail next turns northwest and comes to a footbridge that crosses between the falls' two drops, allowing you to see the smaller falls and the lip of the lower falls. Multicolored leaves float and swirl along the shallow creek.

Minneopa Creek flows 11 miles, most of that through farmland, before reaching park. The Upper Falls drops 8 feet.

After crossing water, the trail goes to the top of the gorge then via limestone steps heads down the ravine's edge. At the bottom is a sandy and rocky trail running along the creek bank.

The orange-red glow of the autumn leaves forms a canopy over the trail. Sugar maple, basswood, elm, and northern red oak, with some hackberry and ironwood, all contribute to the harvest colors. A stand of yellow birch also can be found at the southernmost edge of its range.

How the trail looks in a few decades almost certainly will be different than it does now. Dutch elm disease has claimed most

Autumn colors surround Minneopa Falls near Mankato.

of the elms while oaks, unable to tolerate shade, are not replacing themselves as they fall. The result is maple and basswood steadily becoming more dominant.

At last the trail reaches the Lower Falls. It drops 39 feet and is 25 feet wide. If you can take your hike a couple of days after a thunderstorm, the water flow will be heavier that usual during autumn.

Minneopa Falls exists thanks to millions of years of geology that predates the dinosaurs. Beneath the dirt are several stories of dolomite and sandstone, set down in a shallow sea over tens of millions of years atop a layer of steeply tilted granite. The granite slopes to the east toward Mankato.

At the end of the last ice age about 10,000 years ago, the Glacial River Warren carried meltwater from retreating glaciers, carving out what today is the Minnesota River Valley. As the amount of meltwater decreased, so did the size of the glacial

The now rare American elm grows near Minneopa Creek.

river, leaving dry, flat terraces where it used to flow. The park sits on one such terrace. The Lower Falls at one time likely was the creek's mouth to the Minnesota River. The creek since has eroded away the rock below the waterfall until the mouth moved to its current location, about 2.2 miles downstream.

There's a double waterfall because of three different layers of hardness in the sandstone. The site of each waterfall is the softest while the 66-feet stretch between them is harder or more resistant. The constant spray of the waterfalls ensures nearly vertical gorge walls. Minneopa Falls got its moniker by shortening the Dakota name for it – Minneinneopa – which means "water falling twice."

After taking in the Lower Falls, retrace your steps back to the parking lot.

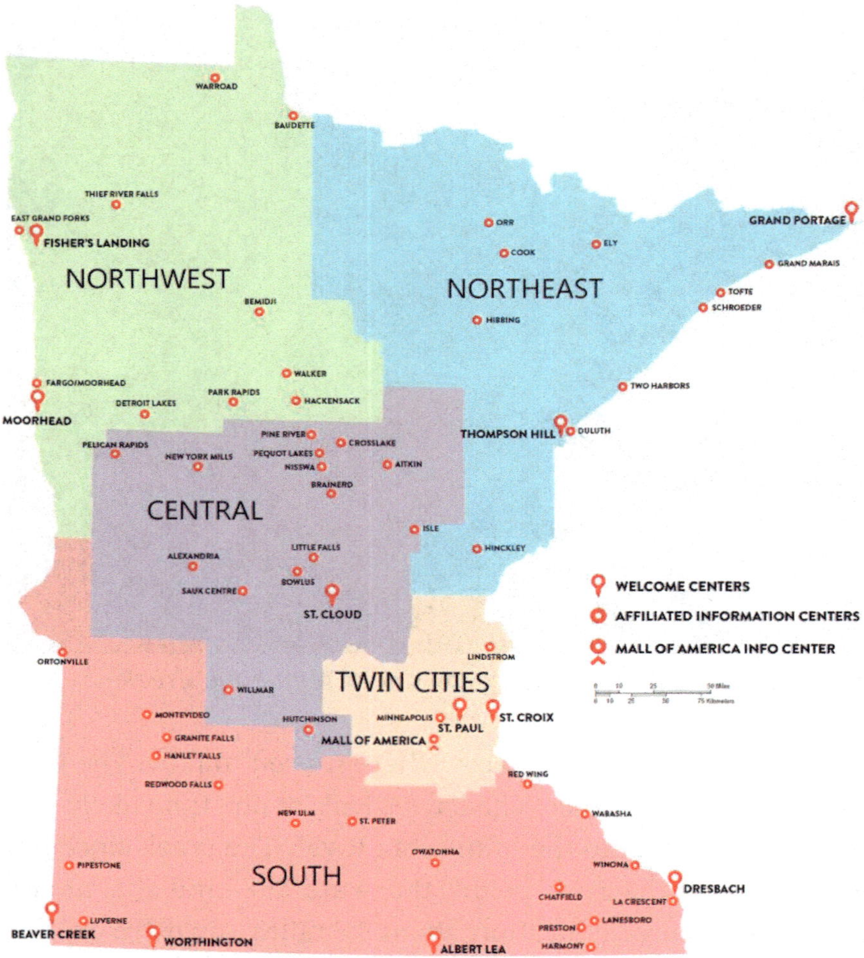

Minnesota's five general regions. Illustration courtesy of Travel Minnesota.

Trails by Region

Every corner of Minnesota offers its own unique take on autumn – from the sugar maple forests of the driftless region to the aspen-oak forests along the Canadian border, from the mixed pine and deciduous forests of the Northwoods to the rare pockets of fiery prairies grasses along the Iowa and Dakota state borders. In Minnesota, you never have to travel far from your home or where you're visiting to enjoy fall colors. Here's a regional list of great hiking spots to see autumn leaves.

Northeast

This region of Minnesota is classic Northwoods country. National and state forests protect much of the area, which stretches from the Lake of the Woods to the Lake Superior shoreline. With much of it at a higher elevation than the rest of the state and the terrain dotted by kettle lakes, it's a perfect destination for fall color lovers.

Tell Lake and Chase Point Trail

Scenic State Park

Day hikers can explore a pine-covered ridge separating two lakes and a woods lit each autumn with colorful leaves at Scenic State Park.

The 2.9-mile route combines two trails – Tell Lake and Chase Point – that are popular at the state park. This route essentially is a lollipop in which you'll do the loop (or Tell Lake Trail) first and then the stem (which is Chase Point Trail).

To reach the trailhead, from Grand Rapids take U.S. Hwy 169 east. Just past Taconite, turn left/north onto County Road 7, also known as Scenic Highway. In about 30 miles, go right/north into the state park on County Road 75. A parking lot is on the road's right side in 0.4 miles. Park there.

From the lot, take the trail going northwest with Coon Lake on the right/northeast and the park entry road on the left/southwest. This is the loop's northern side. It heads through an old-growth maple forest on hills overlooking Coon Lake. Each autumn, its leaves sparkle orange and red.

At 0.3 miles, the trail reaches the information center. Head west across the park entry road and pick up the trail at the interpretive sign near the RV dump station.

Balsam poplar is mainly found in northern Minnesota's wetlands.

A boardwalk crosses a marshy area at about 0.4 miles. You're now on the loop's west side.

Autumn leaves finally arrive at 0.6 miles when the trail enters the woods. The trail turns grassy and wide as heading through a woods of quaking aspen, big-toothed aspen, and balsam poplar.

Quaking aspen is Minnesota's most common tree. When the state's great pineries were clearcut more than a century ago, quaking aspen, as a pioneer species, quickly filled the niche. It reaches between 60 to 100 feet high and is particularly impressive in autumn when the aspen's leaves turn a brilliant gold.

Common throughout the northern part of the state is the big-toothed aspen. It looks similar to the quaking aspen, but the leaf has a blunt, sawtooth-like edge rather than a smooth one. The tree also is a bit shorter, reaching a height of 50-95 feet with a narrow crown. Its bronze autumn leaves flutter in the wind as well, adding a special hue to quaking aspen's waves.

The balsam poplar also is largely confined to the northern part of the state yet even there sticks to edges of streams and wetlands. It's a bit shorter than the quaking and big-toothed aspen, reaching a height of 50 to 80 feet. Its leaves are similarly shaped to the aspen's but has finely toothed edges. The leaves turn yellow in autumn.

After the boardwalk, an overlook with a bench sits on the trail's left side. This is a nice spot to search for osprey, who nest in nearby treetops.

Building their nests out of twigs, osprey prefer the tallest trees near water, where they hunt fish. Majestic looking, an osprey can stretch 25 inches long with a wingspan of up to 6 feet. Rough bumps on the bottom of their feet allow them to grasp slippery fish while a reversible end toe ensures they keep a firm grip on their kill as flying back to the nest. Their wings bend backward so that after a dive they can quickly pull up from the water.

At 0.9 miles, a snowmobile trail crosses the route. Continue straight/east.

After coming up the loop's east side, the trail crosses the park entrance road. The trail then forks; bear right/northeast to along the shore of Coon Lake.

Crystal blue Coon Lake is 340 acres in size. Bluegill, largemouth bass, northern pike and walleye all inhabit its waters, making for great fishing.

After leaving behind Coon Lake, at 1.4 miles, the trail passes a black and spruce bog lined by red and white pines atop a ridge known as an esker. As approaching Sandwick Lake, the trail forks again. Go left/north.

This stem portion of the trail runs along a narrow but high, mile-long esker that separates Sandwick (on the right/east) and Coon (on the left/west) lakes. There are hardly any autumn colors ahead, but the esker between two blue lakes is just too beautiful to skip – the lakes are about 25-30 feet below each side of the trail as sunlight flits through the sweet-scented pines – and since you're this close, why not?

The esker formed at the end of the last ice age, about 10,000 years ago. As the glaciers melted, cracks formed in them, allowing water to drip through and hollow out massive tunnels. The water rushing into these large tunnels carried rocks and sediment. When the glacier fully melted and retreated, the sediment piled at the base of these tunnels was left behind, forming an esker. Plants took root on the long, often serpentine ridges, stabilizing them.

Coon and Sandwick lakes consist of meltwater from ancient glaciers that filled depressions between the esker, probably scooped out by the advancing ice or depressed by the weight of the ice sheet.

At 1.8 miles is a memorial to the park's first superintendent, Hugo V. Kaiser. An island in Sandwick Lake directly to the memorial's east is named after him. You're now halfway up the esker.

Sandwick Lake is slightly smaller than Coon Lake at 254 acres. The two lakes actually are connected by a thin waterway and sometimes are considered one waterbody.

The trail reaches Chase Point at 2.1 miles. Wooden steps head to a deck next to the water, where you'll be treated to a panoramic view of Coon Lake and its pine forest shoreline.

Next, head back south along the esker. At 2.7 miles, when the trail forks, go right/west. In 0.2 miles, you'll arrive back at the parking lot.

Leashed dogs are allowed on the trail. You'll want to carry insect repellent for the boggy part of the hike.

Other Northeast Trails

Carlton County

Hikers can cross a swinging bridge above a raging river running over nearly 2 billion-year old rock then enjoy incredible autumn colors at Jay Cooke State Park. The 1.5-mile round trip East Ridge Trail crosses and then partially follows the St. Louis River southeast of Duluth. To the delight of most kids (and adults), the 219-foot pedestrian bridge bounces and sways. The rest of the trail heads through a hardwood forest. The leaves turn an impressive array of yellows, reds and oranges as autumn sets in. From Interstate 35, take the exit for Minn. Hwy. 210, driving east through Carlton. The park is about five miles from the freeway. Turn right/south at the River Inn Visitor Center and park in the lot nearest the river.

***

Hikers also can walk through a forest of aspen, birch and maple at Jay Cooke State Park. A 2-mile round trip segment of the Organtz Trail can be extended to a 4-mile round trip if doing the other segment; at one time, the trail was a loop, but there's now a gap in it. From Cloquet, take Interstate 35 south. Exit east onto Minn. Hwy. 210, driving through Carlton. Turn right/south into the lot and picnic area for the Oldenburg Point Shelter. Take the trail going northeast and at Trail Intersection Marker 12, continue left-straight/northeast. A second segment of the trail heads right/south from the marker.

Cook County

After Labor Day, Cascade River State Park's birch leaves turn gold, making for an impressive site against the green spruce and fir. The Lookout Mountain Trail, a 3.5-mile loop, takes you through the forest to an overlook 600 feet above the shoreline, offering a view of the Sawtooth Mountain Range and of blue Lake Superior in the distance. From Grand Marais, take Minn. Hwy. 61 south. After crossing the Cascade River, watch for pullout parking lot on the road's right/north side. The trail begins in the lot's northwest corner.

Itasca County

A forest of red oak, sugar maple, and basswood await at Wabu Woods Scientific and Natural Area. You'll need to rely on deer trails and degraded footpaths to work your way through the woods, but the effort is worth it. Large white pines and occasionally yellow birch dot the forest while low-lying areas offer swamp alder and swamp ash amid white cedar, the state's third most common tree. From Grand Rapids, take Minn. Hwy. 38 north. Turn left/west onto County Road 19. After Cedar Springs Road are signs for the natural area on the road's right/north side. Park off the road between the signs and head north into the woods.

Kanabec County

A variety of hardwoods light up Rum River State Forest with harvest colors each autumn. The 6-mile round trip Arctic Trail (listed on some maps as Kanabec Forest Road North) is a great way to enjoy the fall leaves. Maple, oak, ash, elm and basswood cover the upland areas while ash and elm dominate the lowlands. Fall colors usually peak about mid-October. From Mora, take County Road 6 west. At County Road 47, continue straight/west onto 210th Avenue. Go left/south onto County Road 10 then right/west onto County Road 56. Once in the state forest, Arctic Trail is a country lane on the right/north. Park off the road near the intersection.

Koochiching County

Say "boreal forest," and most people think of vast expanses of pine and spruce. In Minnesota, though, paper birch is a major element of the boreal forest, making for spectacular displays of gold leaves atop white trunks against a backdrop of green conifers. A great place to see birch and conifers during autumn is Pine Island State Forest, the largest of Minnesota's 59 state forests. Try the Pine Island 3 Trails, which total 7.5 miles one-way. Autumn leaves usually peak mid to late September on the trail. From International Falls, take U.S. Hwy. 71 south. In Big Falls, turn right/west onto County Road 30. At Gates Corner, go right/north onto Pine Island Road. After passing Fiero Truck Road, watch for the trailhead on the left/east in about 3 miles. Park off the side of the road.

Lake County

A hike though a birch and aspen forest that ends with an incredible view of Lake Superior awaits at Tettegouche State Park. The 1.1-mile round trip Shovel Point Trail is fairly flat as it runs atop billion-year-old rock. Throughout autumn, birds migrate south past the point. From Silver Bay, drive north on Minn. Hwy. 61. After crossing the Baptism River, turn right/southeast into the park entrance. Go straight on the park entrance road and veer left into the northernmost lot. From the lot's southeastern corner, pick up the interpretive trail that heads toward Lake Superior.

***

Autumn is an excellent time to hike George H. Crosby Manitou State Park, as the leaves are lit in gold and red harvest colors. Try the 4.6-mile round trip Humpback Trail, though a shorter 1.2-mile round trip segment is all that's needed for the best vistas. From Silver Bay, take Minn. Hwy. 61 north. Turn left/northwest onto Minn. Hwy. 1. In Finland, turn right/northeast onto Minn. Hwy. 7/Cramer Road. In about eight miles, Hwy. 7 reaches the park entry road; turn right/southeast onto it. Follow the road to its end where it loops back on itself. Use the parking lot there. The trail leaves from the lot's west side into a hardwood forest of birch and maple.

Pine County

Hikers can walk alongside pretty Tamarack River, where a variety of trees light up the trail in autumn. The 3.75-mile out-and-back Tamarack River Trail runs along the river's west side before it flows into the St. Croix River. Rolling terrain features maple, basswood, ash, aspen, oak, and tamarack along with the evergreens Norway, red and white pine. From Sandstone, take County Road 123 east then go straight-left/east on County Road 30. Turn right/south onto County Road 24 and then left/east onto County Road 25. After passing Markville Cemetery, take the next right/south. Park at the Tamarack horse camp and head south on the trail in the St. Croix State Forest.

***

Day hikers can see how the lumberjack era altered the northern Minnesota landscape in the Chengwatana State Forest along the St. Croix River. The 4-mile round trip Redhorse Trail crosses an area where paper birch and bigtooth and quaking aspen largely have replaced yesteryear's white pine. From Pine City, take County Road 8 east. Go left-straight/northeast onto East Cross Lake Road then turn right/east onto County Road 124/Crooked River Road, left/north onto Evergreen Road, and finally right/east onto Chengwatana Road.

When the road splits in the state forest, go left/northeast. A parking lot is at the road's end.

St. Louis County

Autumn leaves alongside billion-year-old rock and a creek sporting several small waterfalls can be found at Congdon Park in Duluth. The 1.2-mile (one-way) Congdon Park Trail follows Tischer Creek, as it makes its way down the bluffs toward Lake Superior. The orange of maple with the yellow of birch and the gorge's red walls feels like you're walking through a rainbow. In Duluth, park in the lot for Mount Royal Market at the corner of Woodland Avenue and East St. Marie Street. Walk East St. Marie Street east, entering the park at the junction with Vermillion Road.

***

A pair of picturesque waterfalls, footbridges, and a walk alongside Chester Creek await hikers on the Chester Park Loop in Duluth. Located near the University of Minnesota-Duluth campus, the 2.4-mile trail is particularly beautiful in autumn when the golden bronze of maple and basswood leaves form a canopy over the path and float upon the creek. In Duluth from West College Street, take North 19th Avenue E southeast. Turn right/west onto W. Kent Road, then right/west onto East Skyline Parkway after the curve right/northwest onto Chester Park Drive. Park off the road then walk back alongside it to East Skyline Parkway and cross the bridge to the trailhead.

***

A young forest of aspen and birch covers the Anchor Lake Wildlife Management Area. A number of easy-to-hike hunter trails crisscross the 216-acre site, which is nestled in a narrow point on Anchor Lake. A dense conifer forest of green and orange-needled tamarack in the wetlands as nearing the lake add splashes of colors to the gold-leaved younger trees. From Eveleth, take U.S. Hwy. 53 south. A small parking lot is on the highway's right/west side directly across the road from the Anchor Lake Rest Stop. Walk the hunter trail south; it soon turns west and heads to connecting trails in the wildlife area.

***

Orange and various hues of yellow and red leaves await hikers at the Laurentian Divide Recreation Area in Superior National Forest. About 5 miles of various connecting trails lead to the top of the rec area's Lookout Mountain, which offers a fantastic vista. Fun fact: Streams on the divide's north slope head to Canada and drain to Hudson Bay while those on south slope flow into either Lake Superior or the Mississippi River. From Virginia, take U.S. Hwy. 53 north. The rec area is on the right/east.

***

Hikers can enjoy a forest of gold, red and orange maple and yellow birch at Maple Hill Park in Hibbing. A 1.2-mile round trip trail heads around the hill's northeast base then makes a steep 80-foot climb up its side to a vista. The hike can be extended by taking other trails around the hilltop and its bottom. From U.S. 169 and Minn. Hwy. 73 in Hibbing, take the latter south. Turn left/east onto Lindquist Road then right/south onto Erickson Road. Park in the lot at the road's end.

***

An aspen and birch forest awaits along the Sturgeon River in Superior National Forest. The 2.5-mile round trip segment of the Sturgeon River Trail heads through the second-growth forest as well as a stand of stately pines. From Chisholm, head north on Minn. Hwy. 73. Turn left/west onto County Road 65. Look for a large parking on the road's right/north side in about

1.2 miles. Take the trail northwest to a shelter.

***

Fall colors can be seen mixed among the pines on the Hiking Club Trail at Lake Vermilion-Soudan Underground Mine State Park. The trail loops 2.4-miles through the park, passing historic mine pits and crosses an old growth forest. From Minn. Hwys. 1/169 in Soudan, turn north onto County Road 4595/ Main Street then right/northwest onto McKinley Park Road into the state park. Leave your vehicle in the main lot.

Northwest

Minnesota's northwestern counties offer an array of landscapes and hence autumn experiences. Floodplain forests hug the Red River and other waterways. Trees common to oak savannas sit in pockets of remnant northern prairies. The tallgrass aspen parkland offers aspen and oak in a transition zone between the Plains and the Northwoods.

Bog Walk

Lake Bemidji State Park

Day hikers can explore the unique fall colors of a bog at Lake Bemidji State Park.

The Bog Walk runs miles 2.4 miles round-trip. A boardwalk takes you through wetlands – with leaves of various shrubs turning yellow while others remain green – to a beautiful lake ringed by trees with orange needles.

To reach the trailhead, from Bemidji, take County Road 19/Lake Avenue NE north. Pretty Lake Bemidji sits to the left/west, and along the way you'll cross the Mississippi River, which this close to its headwaters is just a small, shallow river. At Bass Lake Road NE, turn right/east; this eventually becomes New Bass Road North. At County Road 20/Birchmont Beach Road NE, go left/west. Next, turn left/south onto County Road 414/State Park Road NE and enter the park. At the next junction, go right/south and then take the next left/southeast into the parking area.

From the parking lot, walk alongside the road you just came in on, heading west. Where the road forks to the ranger station, go right/north. You'll cross County Road 414 and pass the campground's western side. Once you pass the second road to

Tamarack brightens the shores of Big Bog Lake in autumn.

the camper cabins, at 0.3 miles, the trail technically begins. Fortunately, the whole route is shaded.

When the trail crosses County Road 20, you've entered wilderness. A couple of trails branch off to the left/northwest, but you'll want to stay on the main trail, which veers right/east.

Most of the trail to this point has been pines with a few hardwoods. The region is a transition zone between the deciduous forests of maple, basswood and oak to the south and the great boreal forest of spruce, fir, paper birch, aspen, and jack pine to the north.

At 0.7 miles, the trail junctions a path going left/north. Continue right-straight/east. Once you pass the bike parking area, you'll come to the quarter-mile boardwalk over a bog.

The bog sits in a tamarack spruce lowland forest. At your feet are a number of fascinating plants you won't see anywhere but a swamp – sheets of sphagnum moss that look solid but actually sit on oversaturated soil and would sway if stepped on...round-leaved sundew and pitcher plants that dine on insects...and if in late spring or early summer the showy blooms of lady's-slipper and Dragon's-mouth orchid that look like they belong in an elegant home's expensive vase rather than a mysterious bog.

On the slightly higher ground around and in the bog, several shrubs and trees grow. The needles of the black spruce – Minnesota's seventh most common tree – provides year-round greenery.

Leaves on the alders growing in the bog also stubbornly remain green through autumn. The multi-stemmed shrub reaches 10-25 feet high and often forms thickets that are impossible to walk through. To identify an alder, look for warty bark, which are signs of a mature shrub.

Or during autumn just look for the green leaves, both on the shrub and the ground. Bacteria on the alder's roots help convert nitrogen to energy, so when there's less sunlight, the plant has no need to drop its leaves to stay alive as deciduous trees do.

Another common shrub along the boardwalk is the bog birch, known by various other names including dwarf birch, low birch, and swamp birch. Its leaves turn yellow in autumn. Growing about 5-8 feet high, bog birch is a clump-forming shrub that colonizes bogs and lakeshores. It requires wet areas and the full sun to thrive.

In 1.2 miles, the trail reaches Big Bog Lake. Tamaracks, a deciduous conifer tree, line the lake. Each autumn, its needles turn orange and fall off, as if they were leaves on maple tree. They rise up to 70 feet tall and with trunks 14-20 inches wide.

After taking in the sites, retrace your steps back to the parking lot.

Other Northwest Trails

Becker County

Golden maples with red oaks and green jack pines await hikers at Smoky Hills State Forest. Any of the trails in the southern half of the 25,000-acre forest – divided by Minn. Hwy. 34 – makes for an excellent autumn hike. Try the 5-mile round trip Navillus Forest Road, some of which is shared with ATVs. From Detroit Lakes, take Hwy. 34 east. At Pine Grove Roadside Park, turn left/north onto Old Mill Road with the parking lot on the right/east. Cross the road onto the trail, which heads south, turning back at Hanna Ore Road.

***

Harvest-hued leaves mixed with conifers await on a segment of the North Country National Scenic Trail. A 5.2-mile one-way hike between 400th Avenue and County Road 26 runs through a transition area from the deciduous woods to the boreal forest. Sugar maple, basswood, aspen, birch and oak mingle with Norway and white pine on a ridge. From Detroit Lakes, take Minn. Hwy. 34 east. Turn left/ north onto County Road 29, then right/east onto County Road 126, and finally left/north onto 400th Avenue. After passing West Island Drive, look for a parking lot on the left/west. Take the trail northeast and arrange for a pickup at the County Road 26 trailhead.

Beltrami County

The vibrant oranges and reds of sugar maples and the golden yellows of basswood await at Lake Bemidji State Park. The 2-mile round trip Rocky Point Trails heads through the hardwood forest alongside the beautiful blue lake. Usually, about half to three-quarters of all the trees have changed color at the park by the first day of fall. From Bemidji, take County Road 19/Lake Avenue NE north. Pretty Lake Bemidji sits to the left/

west, and along the way you'll cross the Mississippi River, which this close to its headwaters is narrow and shallow. At Bass Lake Road NE, turn right/east; this eventually becomes New Bass Road North. At County Road 20/Birchmont Beach Road NE, go left/west. Next, turn left/south onto County Road 414/State Park Road NE and enter the park. After crossing Bass Creek, park in the lot on the right/south. Pick up the trail on the lot's south side; some of it goes southeast but most of it heads northwest to Rocky Point, the highest spot on the lake.

Cass County

Hikers can enjoy great fall colors at Pillsbury State Forest. The 8.2-mile round trip Pillsbury State Forest Trail heads through a mixed forest of gold aspen and basswood, crimson maples and oaks, and green jack and white pine. Half-way through the hike, large, old red pines rise at an old logging road, marking a good turnback spot. From Brainerd, take Minn. Hwy. 210 west. Go right/north onto County Road 18 SW then left/west onto County Road 77 SW. Next, turn left/west onto Pillsbury Forest Road SW and park in the Pillsbury Forest Horse Camp South. The trail heads east from it.

Clay County

Though known more for its tallgrass prairie, Buffalo River State Park also offers great fall colors. Try the 3-mile River View Trail, which loops through a riverine forest of cotton-wood, basswood, elm and ash. From Moorhead, take U.S. Hwy. 10 east. Turn right/south onto County Road 44. From the parking lot, walk south across the picnic area to the River View Trail.

Clearwater County

Autumn colors usually peak the last week of September in

Clearwater County. One great spot to experience them is via the North Country National Scenic Trail heading west to an overlook atop 1,797-foot Tim-Don-Del Hill. A sea of hardwoods in harvest colors stretches south for up to 18 miles on sunny days. The trail runs 2.2 miles round trip and can be steep at spots. From Bagley, go south on Minn. Hwy. 92 then straight/south on Minn. Hwy. 200. Turn right/south onto County Road 39 then left/east onto Cox Lake Road. Go left/east onto Anchor Hill Road then right/south onto Anchor Matson Road. A parking lot is at the trailhead.

Hubbard County

Autumn leaves mixed with evergreens in a transition zone between North America's great deciduous and boreal forests await on the North County National Scenic Trail. An 8-mile one-way segment of the trail runs between Hubbard County Roads 4 and 91. Mixed amid the old-growth white pine and bogs of tamarack and black spruce is young aspen and mature forests of basswood, birch, poplar and oak. From Bemidji, take U.S. Hwy. 71 south. In Lake George, turn left/south onto County Road 4. After passing Halverson Forest Road, look for the trailhead parking lot on the left/east. Take the trail southeast. Arrange for a pickup from the County Road 91 trailhead.

Kittson County

Hikers can enjoy the golden autumn colors of Minnesota's rare aspen-oak forest at Lake Bronson State Park. The 1.75-mile Aspen Parklands Interpretive Trail loops through the ecosystem where prairie meets Northwoods. Interpretive signs along the trail highlights woodland features. From Karlstad, take U.S. Hwy. 59 north. Turn right/east onto County Road 10 then left/north onto County Road 28. Follow County 28 right/

east into the park then head to the Two Rivers Campground. Use the parking lot for horse trailers and walk-in campers.

Lake of the Woods County

Day hikers can walk along the shores of the vast Lake of the Woods while enjoying autumn leaves at Zippel Bay State Park. The 1.3-mile lollipop trail – unnamed but christened the Zippel Bay Trail here for convenience sake – heads through a woods and then along the beach on the 1485-square-mile Lake of the Woods. The golden leaves of willow shimmer in the wind from the open lake, all backed by the gentle swish of russet-leaved oaks, yellow turning to maroon ash trees, and the bronze of birch with jack pine offering a green accent. From Baudette (the self-proclaimed Walleye Capital of the World), take Minn. Hwy. 172 north. Turn left/west onto County Road 8 then right/north onto County Road 34, which heads into the park; a lot is at the road's end. The trail runs north from the lot.

Mahnomen County

A small woodland of oak, maple and aspen light up in harvest colors each autumn at Warren Lake State Wildlife Management Area. A 1-mile round trip trail winds through the heart of the woods, which borders Warren Lake. Deer and forest upland birds inhabit the wildlife area. From Twin Valley, take Minn. Hwy. 32 north. Turn right/east onto Minn. Hwy. 200, then Mahnomen County Road 2 left/north, and lastly Hwy. T47 right/west. Park off the side of the road about 100 feet before the first driveway. The trail is on the road's left/north side.

Marshall County

Bur oak, aspen and cottonwood brighten Old Mill State Park in harvest hues each autumn. The 1.25-mile round trip Painted

Turtle Trail walks under this canopy of fall colors on the Middle River's west side. From the city of Middle River, take Minn. Hwy. 32 south. Turn right/west onto 330th Street NW/County Road 28; continue left-straight/west on 330th Street NW when Hwy. 28 splits. Go right/northwest onto 240th Avenue NW/ County Road 128 then left/west into the park on County Road 40. From the parking lot, head southwest to the Stone Bridge on the Middle River.

Norman County

While known more for its namesake flower, Prairie Smoke Dunes Scientific and Natural Area also is an excellent place to see autumn leaves. The natural area's north side sports basswood and green ash in a particularly dense forest for the prairie. Bur oak dots the surrounding savanna. About 4.7 miles (round trip) of old jeep trails wind through the natural area. From Twin Valley, take Minn. Hwy. 32 north. Turn left/west onto County Road 7. In about 0.66 miles is jeep trail entrance on the right/north; park there.

Pennington County

Autumn leaves can be enjoyed at the wooded Greenwood Trails Recreation Area. A 0.8-mile round trip paved trail runs between Greenwood Street and Pennington Avenue/County Road 17, but a variety of other footpaths wind through the nearly 50-acre park along the Red Lake River. In Thief River Falls, from the junction of Minn. Hwy. 32 and Greenwood Street, take the latter east. After crossing the river, turn right/ south into a parking lot for the park.

Polk County

An aspen-oak woodland awaits hikers during autumn at

Thorson Waterfowl Production Area-Polk County. A 0.95-mile round trip jeep trail runs between County Road 41 and Burnham Creek (the road north of the creek is on private land). In addition to harvest colors, watch for deer, waterfowl, and prairie chickens that call the production area home. From U.S. Hwy. 2 just east of Crookston, take Minn. Hwy. 9 south. Turn left/southeast onto County Road 109 then right/west onto County Road 41. The jeep trail heads north from the road in about a mile.

Roseau County

Each autumn, paper birch brightens the pine-heavy Beltrami Island State Forest in yellow leaves. For great colors, try the 3-mile Bemis Hill Trail, a set of three-stacked loops with three access trails near the Bemis Hill Campground. Other hardwoods also can be found in Minnesota's second largest state forest, with fall foliage usually peaking mid to late September. From Warroad, take County Road 5 south. Turn right/west onto Thompson Forest Road. Turn right/north into the campground for parking; the trail heads northeast from the parking lot.

Wilkin County

Great displays of fall foliage are difficult to find on the prairie, but small patches of woods, especially on shorelines, usually can be located. One such spot is the Lions Park along the Otter Tail River in Breckinridge. From County Road 12 and U.S. Hwy. 75 in Breckingridge, take the latter north. The park's entry is on the right/east side.

Central

Central Minnesota offers a number of great autumn hikes. A transition zone between the Great Plains and the Northwoods, here you can find a little bit of both areas – prairies, oak savannas, wetlands, the Big Woods, and pine forests. It's a bit of a sampler plate of Minnesota ecosystems and the many trees that reside there.

Observation Tower Trail

Mille Lacs Kathio State Park

Hikers can climb a 100-foot observation/fire tower for a fantastic view of Mille Lacs Lake and the surrounding countryside at Mille Lacs Kathio State Park. To reach the tower, you'll hike a series of connecting trails for about two miles through dense woodland in one of the state's most popular parks.

From Onamia, take U.S. Hwy. 169 about 8 miles north of Onamia. At the Kathio Arrowhead sign, turn onto County Road 26. After a mile, you'll come to the park entrance where a small fee is required. Follow the park road past the observation tower. At the first and second intersections, continue driving straight; just past the Ogechie Campground is a parking lot. Pick up the Hiking Club Trail at the lot's northeast end and go right.

The park's 35 miles of trails all are well maintained but easy to get lost on as they meander and frequently intersect. Watch for the trail junction markers to stay on track.

Paralleling the road you just drove in on, continue walking in a roughly eastern direction. At trail junction marker 20, depart the Hiking Club Trail by heading right; you'll then cross the road you came in on.

Autumn colors fill the forest around Mille Lacs, as seen from the state park's observation tower.

The park itself is a section of a terminal moraine, a geological term for where glaciers stopped advancing during the last ice age. The glaciers left behind gravel and boulders carried here from Canada. Upon melting, this region was underwater and slowly has been draining ever since.

At marker 21, go right/south. The collection of trails to the tower route you through a second-growth forest, consisting mainly of aspen, birch, maple and oak. When you spot conifer stands, you're glimpsing what this region looked like more than a century ago before loggers canvassed the area. Closer to the ground in June, you may notice pretty white trilliums blooming.

During autumn, the trail is a fantastic array of harvest colors. The gold and bronzes of aspen and birch blend with the yellows, oranges and reds of sugar and red maples. Oranges and browns of oaks with their plentiful acorns round out the scene.

Go left/east at marker 33. You'll then cross another park road. To give you a sense of where you're at, this is the road that made the second intersection with the park road that you came in on.

At marker 32, go straight/east. Despite the number of trails and roads, by this time you'll probably have noticed the great variety of wildlife in the park. White-tailed deer, squirrels, chipmunks and even black bear scurry about at ground level while high overhead eagles, osprey, Canadian geese, and loons abound. When coming across small clearings and aspen stands, watch for ruffed grouse.

Go straight/east at marker 29. As walking, you may be wondering where the park's name, "Mille Lacs Kathio," comes from. "Mille Lacs" is a French term meaning "1,000 Lakes," which is what early European explorers and fur traders called the region. Blame "Kathio," however, on poor handwriting – when explorer Daniel Duluth wrote that he called the area "Izatys" – which the native Mdewakanton Sioux living here called themselves – the "Iz" looked like a "K." One more error turned "Katys" to "Kathio," which doesn't translate to anything.

At marker 3, go left/north. People have lived in what is now "Kathio" State Park for at least 9,000 years, or since that last ice age ended. In fact, the park can boast that it's one of the most important collections of archeological sites in the state. Nineteen ancient sites have been identified. You can visit one of them when you return to the parking lot where your vehicle is located; the Cooper Site, an ancient Sioux village, is within walking distance and southwest of the parking lot, sitting on the shore of Ogechie Lake.

But first, let's get to the observation tower. At marker 4, go

The crown of the red maple shines brilliantly during autumn.

right/east. In this area, watch your step: Some trails are for both equestrian riders and backpackers, so be careful of horse manure that sometimes is on the path. You'll cross another park road (which leads to the first intersection with the park road that you came in on). You'll then come upon marker 5; continue straight to the observation tower.

The Civilian Conservation Corps constructed the Isle Harbor tower in 1936, and it was moved to the park in 1982. Anyone can go up it during daylight, but be aware that the open stairways makes this unsuitable for young children, who easily could fall or be scared; older children, teens, and the height-averse certainly may find it a worthy challenge as well. The views from the top make it worthwhile, though.

Return the way you came. If you have the whole day, the park offers picnic areas, swimming beaches, a visitor center, and several quality interpretive/nature programs.

Other Central Trails

Aitkin County

Among the best spots in Minnesota to see fall colors is Savanna Portage State Park. Its fairly flat 4.25-mile Continental Divide loop heads through a forest of tall maple, oak, poplar and birch sprinkled heavily with white and red pine. From McGregor, take Minn. Hwy. 65 north. Turn right/east onto County Road 14; it becomes Lake Place upon entering the park. Leave your vehicle in the parking lot on the left/west just before Loon Lake Road. Cross Lake Place and take the Old Schoolhouse Trail north. Make it a loop by going right/south onto the Continental Divide Trail then right/west onto the Anderson Road Trail, which leads back to your trailhead.

Benton County

A pin and bur oak woodlands can be enjoyed at Englund Ecotone Scientific and Natural Area. You'll need to rely on game trails and degraded footpaths to get through the forest, though. Still, the hike is worth it, as this is one of the few remaining natural areas in a rapidly urbanizing county. From Foley, take Minn. Hwy. 25 north. Turn left/west onto Little Rock Road, left/south on U.S. Hwy. 10, and then left/east onto 85th Street NW. When 85th Street splits, take it right/southeast. The road ends at the natural area.

Crow Wing County

Colorful maple, oak and aspen line the riverbank at Crow Wing State Park. The 3.2-miles round trip Hiking Club Trail runs roughly in a loop, mostly along the Mississippi River. Historic sites, wildlife, and a picnic area can be found along the way. From Brainerd, take Minn. Hwy. 371 south. Turn right/northwest onto County Road 27 into the park. The county road ends at your parking lot, from which the trail goes north.

Douglas County

A segment of the Central Lakes Trail heads through colorful woodlands and past blue lakes. The paved four-mile round trip hike is a bicycle path open to hikers. Leaves often cover the trail by mid-autumn. From the junction of County Roads 82 and 22 in Alexandria, take the latter northwest. Turn left/southwest onto Lake Cowdry Road NW. After crossing the trail, the parking lot is on the right/northwest. Walk the trail northwest. Turn back at Centennial Drive NW.

***

Maple, basswood and aspen in their full autumn glory can be seen at Lake Carlos State Park. The 2-mile round-trip Maple-Basswood Interpretive Trail heads through the heart of the park across gently rolling hills. From Alexandria, take Minn. Hwy. 29 north. Turn left/west onto County Road 38 and once in the park go right/north onto County Road 62. When County Roads 38 and 62 split, take the former left/west. Park in the lot at the road's end. Walk west on the trail that skirts Hidden Lake's north shore.

Grant County

Among the best places to find autumn colors in the prairie is near water. The Frikken Waterfowl Production Area is one such spot with a tree grove along its northern side near a pond and wetlands that attracts birds. A jeep trail runs about 0.7-miles round trip through the production area. From Elbow Lake, take U.S. Hwy. 59 north. Turn right/east onto County Road 26 then right/south onto County Road 51. In about 0.3 miles, look for a driveway on the road's left/east side. Park off the side of the road and walk straight east to the tree grove.

Kandiyohi County

Hikers can enjoy a panoramic view of fall colors at Sibley State Park. The 3.3-mile Mt. Tom Trail (also known as the Hiking Club Trail) loops through the center of the park's oak woods as ascending a hill about 200 feet above the surrounding terrain. From Wilmar, drive north on U.S. Hwy. 71. Enter the park by going left/west onto County Road 48 then taking a right/north onto the road to the park office. Past the office, the road splits; go right/east and park in the interpretive center lot at the road's end. The trail heads northwest from the lot.

***

A visit to Prairie Woods Environmental Learning Center offers a two-for-one fall color experience – the brilliant purples of prairie grasses and the autumn leaves of maples, oaks and basswoods on the hills. Try the 0.56-mile Kemp Trail, which circles a pond through the woods while dipping briefly into the prairie. From Willmar, take U.S. Hwy. 71 north. Turn left/west onto 122nd Avenue NE/County Road 29. Follow Hwy. 29 when it curves right/north. Go left/west onto the learning center and leave your vehicle at the Trailhead Building.

McLeod County

Autumn colors await at a small woods in Swan Lake County Park. A 0.55-mile round trip trail runs alongside the woods and past an oak savanna. From Hutchinson, take Minn. Hwy. 7 east. Turn left/north onto County Road 4, right/east onto County Road 79, left/north onto Kildeer Avenue, then right/northeast into Swan Lake Road. The park entry is on the left/north. The trail leaves from the parking area's northwest corner.

Meeker County

A small woodlands brightens the prairie in autumn colors at

the Harvey Waterfowl Production Area. A 0.15-mile one-way path passes trees and leads to the woods near a large pond frequented each fall by migrating birds. Extend the trail into the woods via game trails and degraded footpaths. From Willmar, take U.S. Hwy. 12 east. Turn left/north onto 560th Avenue then right/east onto 290th Street. The entry to the waterfowl area is in 0.66 miles on the right/south; park along the road.

Mille Lacs County

A beaver pond surrounded by beautiful fall colors await hikers at Mille Lacs Kathio State Park. The 1.2-mile Glacial Ridge Trail loops through hilly terrain, featuring ash, basswood, maple, aspen and tamarack, as well as some evergreens. Wooden bridges add charm to the autumn hike. From Onamia, take Minn. Hwy. 27 west. Turn right/north on County Road 26/Shakopee Lake Road. Go left/west on Kathio State Park Road and leave your vehicle at the RV Sanitation Station. The trail is at the lot's northeast corner.

Morrison County

An upland forest of mature oak, big-toothed aspen, and birch await hikers at Lake Alexander Woods Scientific and Natural Area. The woodland sits on the higher ground that weaves around small lakes and wetlands, a classic example of central Minnesota's kettle and knob topography. There are no maintained trails in the natural area, so you'll have to rely on game trails and degraded footpaths to wend through the woods, which is quite colorful in autumn. From Little Falls, take U.S. Hwy. 10 northwest. In Cushing, turn right/north onto Bison Road then right/northeast onto County Road 5/Bear Road. Park in the grassy driveway for the natural area on the road's left/west side.

Otter Tail County

An array of autumn leaves surround the sides of and plains below Rustling Leaf Mountain at Inspiration Peak State Wayside Park. A 0.5-mile trail heads up the "mountain," which rises 400 feet above the countryside. While the route up is under a canopy of harvest-hued leaves, the top is a prairie that on clear days offers a 20-mile view around. About 50 lakes, many surrounded by hardwoods, sit in that circle. From Fergus Falls, take Minn. Hwy. 210 east. Turn right/south onto County Road 5 then left/east on County Road 38. When the road curves south, go left/northeast onto 435th Avenue then right/east onto 120th Street.

Pope County

Hikers can cross a terrain shaped during the last ice age and enjoy autumn colors because of it. The 4.8-mile Mountain Lake Trail at Glacial Lakes State Park features a kame, rolling hills, and kettle lake. Yellow-leaved basswood and russet-colored oaks thrive on the kame, a hill created when a melting glacier deposited sediment, while crimson sumac, golden quaking aspen, and orange wild plum fill the flat spaces between the low hills. From Starbuck, take Minn. Hwy. 20 south. Go left-straight/south on County Road 41, which curves left/east into the park. Once past the entrance station, take the third left/east and park in the lot at the road's end.

Sherburne County

Autumn colors brighten much of the 427-acre Woodland Trails Regional Park in Elk River. More than six miles of dedicated hiking trails head through the forest there. Use the Green Trail (not its official name but the trail's color on city maps), a set of seven connected loops that runs through the heart of the woods. From the junction of U.S. Hwys. 169 and 10 in Elk River, take the latter west. Turn right/north onto Proctor Avenue NW, which becomes Elk Lake Road NW. Go right/east into the park at the County Road 32 intersection. From the parking lot, walk the Blue Trail east to the Green Trail.

***

Harvest hues abound at the confluence of the Mississippi and Elk rivers in Bailey Point Nature Preserve. Two stacked loops offer about 0.75-miles of trails at the new park. The loops head through and alongside woodlands, which border a savanna that is being restored. From the junction of U.S. Hwy. 10 and Main Street NW in Elk River, take the latter west. Turn left/south onto Morton Avenue NW, which ends in a parking lot at the preserve. The trail heads west from the lot.

***

A profuse array of autumn leaves await at Clear Lake Scientific and Natural Area. Northern red oak, white oak, northern pin oak, with some bur oak and red maple, dominate the canopy. A southern terrace forest along the Mississippi River boasts American elm, box elder, silver maple, green ash, hackberry and basswood. You'll have to rely on game trails and degraded footpaths to traverse the site. From Elk River, take U.S. Hwy. 10 west. In Clear Lake, turn left/southwest onto County Road 24, then right/west onto 90th Street SE, and finally 58th Avenue South. Watch for the natural area's driveway on the road's right/west side; park there.

Stearns County

Walkers can enjoy the reflection of autumn colors off of the Mississippi River at Munsinger and Clemens Gardens. A 1.25-mile round trip walking path runs north-south through Munsinger Gardens with a spur to Clemens Gardens. St. Cloud State

University sits on the river's opposite shore. From the junction of U.S. Hwy. 10 and Third Street SE in St. Cloud, take the latter southwest. Turn left/south onto Wilson Avenue SE, then right/west onto Seventh Street SE, and lastly left/south onto Riverside Drive. Park along Riverside south of 10th Street SE; the gardens are west of the street.

***

Scarlet and golden leaves with tinges of orange await hikers at Quarry Park and Nature Preserve. The 2.3-mile Quarry Park Outer Loop circles the preserve's perimeter, staying in the woods almost the entire way. Fall colors typically peak late September to early October. In St. Cloud, from the southern junction of Minn. Hwys. 15 and 23, take the latter southwest. Turn left/south onto 28th Avenue then left/east onto County Road 137. The preserve's entrance is on the right/south.

***

A diverse array of autumn leaves await hikers at Birch Lake State Forest. A 1.7-mile round trip unnamed lollipop trail heads through a forest of oak, red maple, ironwood, birch and aspen. From Melrose, take County Road 13 north. Turn right/east onto County Road 17, left/north onto Birch Lake Road then right/east onto Birch Lake State Forest Road. Park in the first lot, for campsites 30-35. At the first trail intersection, go straight/west then at the next intersection go left/east.

***

For fall color lovers, late September to early October is an excellent time to hike the Lake Wobegon Trail. During a two-week stretch, sugar maple, ash, aspen and staghorn sumac usually are at their peak along the former rail line turned hiking/bicycling trail. A stretch of the flat trail that is mostly wooded and away from busy Interstate 94 is the 6.4-mile round trip segment between downtown Albany to Peach Drive

Maple leaves begin to change color during early fall in St. Cloud.

at Avon Hills Forest Scientific and Natural Area. In Albany, park along Fifth Street between Railroad and Church avenues, then take the trail east.

***

A vast woods of red and white oak await hikers at Saint John's University's Abbey Arboretum. The 3-mile Chapel Walk heads through a colorful autumn forest with the leaves reflecting off the crystal blue surface of Lake Sagatagan. The trail starts on the beach at the lake's northwest side and runs to Stella Maris Chapel. Legend says that if you're a Bennie – a student at the neighboring College of Saint Benedict – walking with a Johnnie, in the future you'll end up in the chapel exchanging marriage vows. From Interstate 94 northwest of St. Joseph, exit south onto St. John's Road. Turn left/east onto Prep School Road then right/west onto Water Tower Road. Park in one of the spots off the street then walk west and go left/south onto Beach Fire Lane to the lake.

Stevens County

Thanks to several large, low-lying ponds, Stevens County boasts a number of waterfowl production areas. Most lack trees, but one exception is the Hancock WPA, which is split by 280th Street. After a good freeze, the edges of the production area south of the street usually can be traversed. In addition to the autumn leaves, you'll be treated to migrating birds flying in and out of the pond. From Glenwood, take Minn. Hwy. 29 south. Turn right/west onto County Road 2, which naturally becomes County Road 8. In Hancock, turn right/north onto Minn. Hwy. 9 then right/east onto 280th Street. Park off the side of the road and walk south around the pond.

Todd County

An aspen-oak woods offers some rare fall leaf colors on the prairie at Burleene Wildlife Management Area. A 0.23-mile round trip jeep trail runs to the woods on the wildlife area's south side. The hike can be extended via game trails and degraded footpaths. From Long Prairie, take County Road 38 west. Turn right/north on County Road 1 then right/east onto 290th Street. Look for a driveway into the wildlife area on the road's left/north side. Park in the driveway and walk north.

Wadena County

In an area more known for its jack pine, hikers can enjoy an oak woodland at Yaeger Lake Wildlife Management Area. About 1.5 miles of four stacked loops heads through the oak woods on Yaegar Lake's northeast side. From Wadena, travel north on U.S. Hwy. 71. Turn right/east onto County Road 13, then right/east onto County Road 15. In about 0.95 miles, look for a driveway on the road's right/south side. Park in the driveway and walk south onto the stacked loops.

Twin Cities

Though among the 20 largest U.S. metro areas, the Twin Cities has done an impressive job of preserving natural environments through parks and preserves. Because of this, Twin Cities residents and visitors never are far from a good fall color hike. Most of the trails here pass through deciduous forests or marshes where a number of trees and shrubs thrive, but there also are a few apple groves that offer an old farm harvest feel.

South River Bluff Trail

Carpenter Nature Center

Day hikers can enjoy a walk down a bluff to the St. Croix River and then through an apple orchard at the Carpenter St. Croix Valley Nature Center in the southeast Twin Cities.

A nonprofit aimed at preserving wildlife habitat and providing educational opportunities about nature, Carpenter St. Croix Valley is free and offers a number of quality programs through the year. The facility is open every day in autumn from 8 a.m. to 4:30 p.m.

The South River Bluff Trail and a paved trail connecting it to the visitor center runs about 0.95-miles round trip to the shores of the St. Croix. This trail heads through the heart of the center's 425-acre main property in Minnesota; a separate 300-acre restored prairie and wooded bluffs are on a nature preserve in Wisconsin.

To reach the nature center, from U.S. Hwy. 10 take Minn. Hwy. 21 (aka as St. Croix Trail) north and watch for the signs; the center is on the right/east in about two miles. Once on the center's entry road, park in the northern lot.

Check out the interpretive center northeast of the parking

lot for several exhibits and displays about the Lower St. Croix Valley. A paved trail departs from the center's north side.

River shore

Follow the trail east, avoiding the turnoffs onto other paths (Save them for a later visit!). Most of this area is open, so be sure to don suntan lotion or wear a sunhat during summer.

The trail soon curves south; at each of the next three trail junctions, continue heading south. A wetlands is to the east/left with a tree line in the distance that turns an array of reds, yellows and browns each autumn.

Soon the pathway makes a hairpin turn north and reaches the unpaved South River Bluff Trail. Take this down the ridge to the river's edge, which is on the other side of the Railroad Bed Trail. Upon reaching the river, you're about halfway through the hike. The far shoreline is Wisconsin.

The St. Croix River there is close to its widest before flowing into the Mississippi River just a couple of miles south in Prescott, Wis. For the next 123 miles to the north, the river forms the Wisconsin-Minnesota border then meanders into the Badger State for its last 44 miles.

Apple orchard

Upon taking in the great views, turn back, going the way you came. However, if it's autumn, at the next junction after making the hairpin turn north, go left/west. The trail passes through a small wooded area, then heads south into the apple orchard.

Thirteen varieties of apples grow in the orchard. For most apple trees, leaves turn yellow then brown right after the harvest. Fortunately for autumn leaf lovers, the harvest is staggered over 10 weeks.

Apple picking season begins in late August with the Zestar!

Zestar! apples were developed in Minnesota and have been available since 1999.

brand ripening. But the light show really begins in early to mid-September when the chestnut crab with its showy red apples and the SweeTango – a brand invented by University of Minnesota scientists through crossing Honeycrisp and Zestar! – are fully ripe.

That makes mid to late September a great time to enjoy the orchard. By then, the chestnut crab and SweeTango leaves have yellowed while McIntosh, Haralson, Honeycrisp and Sweet 16 apples all are ripe. The Sweet 16 is particularly impressive, bearing red showy apples with hints of light green that grow in abundance on each tree.

The show continues in late September and early October, as leaves have yellowed on the aforementioned quartet while the Cortland, Honey Gold, Connell Red and Regent apples all have ripened. Honey Gold is yellow skinned with russet dots while the Connell Red is a solid orange-red color.

By mid-October, apple picking is nearing its end with Cortland, Honey Gold, Connell Red and Regent leaves yellow but only the SnowSweet ripening. It bears a bronze-red blush-colored fruit.

The season ends in late October with just the Keepsake variety ripening and the SnowSweet's leaves turning color. By then, leaves from most other trees have thinned out.

Staying on the orchard's west side, the trail exits into the Apple Shack, which sells apples and honey grown at the center, as well as food ranging from pumpkins and squash to jams and syrups.

Leave through the Apple Shack's other side into the southern parking lot. Follow this back to the northern parking lot and your vehicle.

Other Twin Cities Trails

Anoka County

Cottonwood, basswood and maples make for a beautiful autumn walk at Rum River Central Regional Park in Anoka. The 3.25-mile Rum River Trail loops through the park's riverine forest; about half of the trail parallels the Rum River. From U.S. Hwy. 10 in Anoka, take Seventh Avenue north. After crossing the Rum River, turn right/east onto Park Road. When the road splits in the park, go right/south. Leave your vehicle in either of the next two parking lots; the trail runs alongside them.

***

Maple and oak trees line the paths at Pioneer Park in Blaine. A loop and the two stems to it run about 0.8-miles round trip. About half of the 100-acre city park is an upland woods with most of the trails paved. From Minn. Hwy. 65 and 125th Avenue NE in Blaine, take the latter east. The park's main entrance and a parking lot is on the left/north.

***

A canopy of colorful autumn leaves covers a pathway that almost fully loops Highland Lake at Kordiak Park in Columbia Heights. A 1.5-mile trail heads around the lake's south, west and north sides as well as runs to adjoining streets. From Central Avenue NE in Columbia Heights, take 49th Avenue NE east. The parking lot is on the avenue's left/north side after passing Fairway Drive NE.

***

Majestic burr and red oak groves await hikers at Bunker Hills Regional Park. A 2.5-mile paved loop is especially stately in autumn when the bur oak turns a golden yellow-brown and the red oak various shades of crimson, burgundy, yellow and orange. A few paper birches, whose white trunks support amber-colored leaves, can be found near the marshy sections. From the intersection of U.S. Hwy. 10 and Main Street NW in Coon Rapids, take Main Street east; turn left/north onto County Road A and park in the lot on the right/east side of the highway just before the junction with County Road B. Pick up the trail from the lot's northwest side. The loop runs north/east of County A, east and north of County B, and south of Bunker Lake.

***

Hikers can head through an oak woodland at Innsbruck Nature Center in Fridley. A roughly 2-mile round trip trail loops around a small pond and heads to the center's far corners. Interpretive signs along the way tells about Innsbruck's birds, wetlands, geology and more. From Minn. Hwy. 65 in Fridley, go east on Mississippi Street NE. Turn right/south onto Central Avenue NE, then left/east onto Gardena Avenue NE, and finally right/south onto Arthur St. NE. The nature center is on the left/east.

***

Walkers can enjoy a paved path lined with fall foliage at Lakeside Lions Park. The 0.35-mile loop partially heads alongside Spring Lake. From Mounds View Boulevard in Spring Lake Park, take Pleasant View Drive south. The park is south of Hillview Road.

Carver County

An incredible variety of trees – and autumn colors – can be seen at the Minnesota Valley State Recreation Area. The 3.8-mile Lawrence Trail heads through ash, box elder, and oaks, enters a stand of ironwood and box elder, crosses a highland of bur oak, basswood and ash, and traverses stands of tall aspen and stately oaks. From Jordan, take U.S. Hwy. 169 northeast. Turn left/north onto County Road 57/Park Boulevard then left/north to the park's trail center.

***

Hikers can enjoy the reflections of autumn colors as walking around tree-lined McKnight Lake. A 1.8-mile trail loops around the lake and, should you wish to go farther, connects to other paths. From the junction of U.S. Hwy. 212 and Minn. Hwy. 41/ North Chestnut Street in Chaska, take the latter north. Turn left/west onto West 82nd Street then left/south onto McKnight Road. Watch for a dirt path going east and park off the side of the road there.

***

Autumn colors and a harvest vibe abound at Gale Woods Farm near Minnetrista. A 2.1-mile limestone trail rambles through the park's rolling hills and past two lakes and a working farm featuring sheep, pigs, cows and more. From Victoria, take Minn. Hwy. 7 west. Turn right/north onto County Road 44 then left/west onto County Road 110. Go left/north east onto

County Road 11 (Extended) into the park.

***

A colorful maple and oak forest await day hikers at the Carver Park Reserve. The 4.8-mile Lundsten Lake Loop passes two lakes as winding through the forest. A bridge crosses part of Lundsten Lake, offering beautiful reflections of the harvest-hued canopy. From Minn. Hwy. 5 in Victoria, take County Road 11/Victoria Drive north then turn left/southwest onto Carver Park Road. Park where the road ends in a roundabout.

Chisago County

The southernmost section of Minnesota Interstate State Park offers a number of great day hiking trails to explore the Dalles of the St. Croix. To reach the area, from U.S. Hwy. 8 turn east onto Milltown Road. A parking lot is at the end of the entry road. Along the parking lot's northwest side are three trailheads. The Sandstone Bluff Trail heads northwest under Hwy. 8 to a nice vista of the valley and river gorge below. A 1-mile lollipop trail, it's spectacular in autumn with a mix of colors from the orange maples, red sumac and brilliant yellow oaks.

***

Wild River State Park offers two great autumn trails. The 1.5-mile River Terrace Loop and its stem trail circles through a bottomland forest of silver maple and basswood along the St. Croix River. The 4.6-mile Sunrise Loop on the park's north side is little used and so offers lots of solitude as it runs along the St. Croix; silver maple, ash, black willow and cottonwood all thrive there. From North Branch, take Minn. Hwy. 95 east/south. For the River Terrace Loop, turn onto and take County Road 12 to the park entrance, then follow the main park road to a parking lot near the picnic area. For the Sunrise Loop, from Hwy. 95 turn left/north on County Road 9, taking it into the hamlet of

Sunrise; go right/north on Ferry Road into the park. When the road runs out, use the parking lot on the left/west. Hike Ferry Road south to the trailhead and cross Ferry Road (which leads to the boat landing) then over the Sunrise River footbridge. On the other side of the bridge, the loop begins.

***

Hikers can follow some of the same footpaths and rail lines that the region's first Swedish immigrants used to settle Chisago County and Minnesota on the Swedish Immigrant Trail. During the late 1800s, many Swedish immigrants took the ferry across the St. Croix River and then footpaths to their destinations. A spur off the St. Paul-Duluth rail route to Wyoming opened during 1880, helping speed the immigration in-land. Perhaps the best of the trail's completed portions is the Shafer Segment, which runs roughly west of the hamlet through wooded areas and past bucolic landscapes. Birch trees dominate in some sections, but the trail is mainly lined by mixed hardwoods that leave the path and its grass shoulders covered in an array of colorful leaves during autumn. Park on the street in downtown Shafer, off of Redwing Avenue near 303rd Street. The trailhead is near 303rd and heads for about two miles east of Redwing. Look for the white signs with the trail logo in the blue and yellow colors of Sweden's flag.

Dakota County

Autumn colors light up heavily wooded Alimagnet Park in Apple Valley. A 2.25-mile round-trip trail runs through the park; it includes a spur to pretty Alimagnet Lake, where the tree colors reflect off the water on sunny days. From County Road 42 in Apple Valley, take Garden View Drive north. Turn left/west onto Walnut Lane then right/north onto Ridgeview Drive. The road ends at small parking lot with the trail heading north into the woods.

***

Various shades of tan, orange and red leaves brighten the canopy at Terrace Oaks West Park. The 3.2-mile Terrace Oaks Trail loops through the 230-acre woodland. The trail is mostly shaded; on sunny days as fall colors peak, you'll feel like you're walking through an orange tunnel. From County Road 42 in Burnsville, take Interstate 35E north. Exit left/north onto County Road 11 then turn right/east into the Terrace Oaks' parking lot. The trail heads east from the lot's center and northeast corner.

***

Maple, birch, willow, and box elder brighten the deep, narrow gorge at Miesville Ravine Park in harvest hues. A 1.54-mile round trip trail runs through the ravine alongside Trout Brook, a tributary of the Cannon River. The ravine is thickly wooded and almost entirely shaded. From Cannon Falls, take Minn. Hwy. 20 north. Turn right/east onto 280th Street. Once in the park after crossing the stream, go left/north onto a dirt road that leads to a parking lot.

***

Day hikers can enjoy modern sculptures in a forest setting at the Caponi Art Park in Eagan. A variety of pathways walk through the 60-acre site that in autumn is made all that magical by the changing leaves of birch, maple and basswood. Most of the sculptures were created by Italian-born Anthony Caponi, who as an adult adopted Minnesota as his home. From Interstate 35 in Eagan, take Diffley Road east. Turn right/southeast and park in the lot. The art park is on both sides of the highway with an underpass connecting them.

***

Autumn colors light up Jim Bell Park and Preserve on Farmington's northeast side. About 1.3 miles of trails run between a woods and two ponds at the preserve. From County Road 64 and Pilot Knob Road in Farmington, take the latter north. Turn right/east onto 194rd Street West. When the street becomes Dunbury Avenue, park on the side of the street at the wooded area. The trail heads right/southeast from the street into the preserve.

***

Maple and ash trees along with some quite large oaks await hikers at Spring Lake Park Reserve. A 3-mile trail loops through a woods atop a bluff on the Mississippi River. Moss-covered rocks and birch accent the mostly maple forest. From Hastings, take Second Street west. When the street splits, go right/northwest onto Niniger Road, which naturally becomes 132nd Street East. Turn right/north onto Idell Avenue, which becomes 127th Street East when it curves west. Head right/north onto the park entry road and leave your vehicle in the lot for the playground. The connector trail heads east from the parking lot.

***

Maple and birch stands await hikers at Ritter Farm Park in Lakeville. The 3.2-mile Mader Loop combined with the Matterhorn Trail heads through then skirts the park's woodlands. From the junction of Interstate 35 and 185th Street/County Road 60 in Lakeville, take the latter east. Turn right/south onto Kendrick Avenue, right/west onto 195th Street West, then right/north onto Ritter Trail. At the second split in the park road, go left/northwest. The road ends in a parking lot with the trail leaving from the north side.

***

Gold aspen and russet oak leaves await hikers at Vermillion Highlands Wildlife Management Area. The 4.6-mile Wetland

and Pine Loop largely stays in the woods while circling a wetlands that drains into the Vermillion River. The wildlife area covers more than 2800 acres. From County Road 42 and Minn. Hwy. 3 in Rosemount, take the latter south. Turn left/ east onto County Road 46 then right/south onto Clayton Avenue. A parking lot for the trailhead is on the right/west.

***

At Thompson County Park, hikers can explore a forest similar to that which existed before pioneers arrived in the area. The 1.4-mile Thompson Trail loops through a maple and oak woodlands as well as circles a small lake. Egrets, mallards and warblers can be seen at the park during the annual autumn migration. From U.S. Hwy. 52 in South St. Paul, exit west onto Butler Avenue and drive into West St. Paul. Turn left/south onto Stassen Lane and park near the activity center.

Hennepin County

Orange and beige oak trees along the Mississippi River can be enjoyed at East River Flats Park in Minneapolis. The 3.75-miles round trip East River Flats Trail runs through a gorge featuring 25-foot high limestone bluffs just below the University of Minnesota. From Interstate 94 between downtown Minneapolis and St. Paul, exit onto Huron Boulevard. Turn left/ east onto Fulton Street; at East River Parkway, go straight-right/west, and finally head left/south into the East River Flats Park parking lot. Walk the trail southeast, turning back at the Old Wagon Road Trail junction.

***

An oak and maple woods awaits hikers at Bryant Lake Regional Park. A 1.3-mile trail consisting of the park's two southernmost loops partially runs alongside Bryant Lake. Cottonwoods and ash trees flourish on lower ground. From the junction of Interstate 494 and U.S. Hwy. 212 in Eden Prairie, take the latter northeast. Exit left/northwest onto Shady Oak Road. Turn left/southwest onto Old Shady Oak Road, which naturally becomes Rowland Road. Go left/southwest onto Bryant Lake Regional Access road and enter the park. Take the first left/south and park in the second lot. The trail heads west south of the lot.

***

Shady woodlands await hikers at Lake Minnetonka Regional Park. A 1.8-mile trail, most of it unpaved, heads through a thick forest of tall trees. From Chanhassen, take Minn, Hwy. 5 west. Turn right/north onto Rolling Acres Road, a left/west onto Minn. Hwy. 7, then a right/north onto County Road 44. The park entry is on the right/east. Go right/southeast onto Old County Road and park in the first lot. Walk the road northwest then go left/west onto Minnetrista Regional Trail. The woods is on the other side of County Road 44.

***

Dense growths of maple and oak can be enjoyed at Crow-Hassan Regional Park near Rogers. While much of the park is savanna, a 6-mile round trip trail can be taken along the edge of the Crow River, where most of the trees grow. From the junction of Interstate 94 and Minn. Hwy. 101 in Rogers, take the latter south. Turn right/south onto Main Street/County Road 150. Go right/west onto County Road 49, which becomes Tucker Road. Next, head right/northwest onto Territorial Road/County Road 116 then left/southwest onto Hassan Parkway, and right/northwest onto Ghostley Road. At Park Drive, continue straight/west into the park. From the parking lot, walk west toward the trees.

***

Yellow aspen and tan-orange oak leaves await hikers at Elm

Creek Park Reserve in Dayton. Try the 4.5-mile Orange Loop (so-named here because of its color on reserve maps) that runs southeast of the Eastman Nature Center. The trail crosses both Elm and Rush creeks in the 4900-acre reserve. Keep an out for wildlife, including eagles, white-tailed deer, loons, and hawks. From Dayton River Road in Dayton, take Pineview Lane south. Go right/west onto County Road 121 then left/east onto Elm Creek Road into the reserve. When the reserve road splits, head right/south. Park at the nature center.

Isanti County

Hikers can enjoy the colorful autumn leaves of red oak, aspen, red maple and birch beneath a supercanopy of white pine at Twin Lakes Scientific and Natural Area. No maintained hiking trails run through the 48-acre site that wraps around Horseshoe Lake's southeastern shore, but the understory is remarkably open, allowing for easy bushwhacking. From Cambridge, take Minn. Hwy. 65 south. Turn left/east onto County Road 9. Twin Lakes is between Mulenberg and Vassar streets on the road's north side. Park off the side of the road and enter at any opening in the woods.

Ramsey County

Tan-colored oak and yellow-leaved birch await hikers at Battle Creek Regional Park in Maplewood. The 1.5-mile Battle Creek Loop passes tree-lined ponds and crosses ridgelines overlooking oak-filled gullies. From Interstate 94 east of St. Paul, exit right/south onto White Bear Avenue then turn left/east onto Upper Afton Road. Go right/south onto Winthrop Street then right/west into the park's lot.

***

Two rivers reflect fall colors, as you pass beneath a harvest-hued canopy at Fort Snelling State Park. The 3-mile Pike Island Trail loops around the isle at the confluence of the Mississippi and Minnesota rivers with historic Fort Snelling on the bluff above. Cottonwood, silver maple, ash, and willow trees all thrive on the island. From the junction of Minn. Hwy. 5 and Post Road near Minneapolis-St. Paul International Airport, take the latter southeast. Turn left/northeast onto Snelling Lake Road. Park in the lot when the road runs out. Head northeast on Snelling Lake Trail and at the first junction go right/southeast onto Pike Island Trail.

***

Maple, oak and basswood line the bluff overlooking the Mississippi River in the heart of the state's largest metro area. The Mississippi Gorge Trail loops 7 miles between Ford Parkway and Franklin Avenue with part of the route in Hennepin County. From Ford Parkway in St. Paul, exit north onto Mississippi River Boulevard just east of the waterway. Go north and park at the scenic overlook on the left/west just past Woodlawn Avenue. The trail is on the overlook's west side. Cross the river at the Franklin Avenue bridge, continue south through Minneapolis, then cross back into St. Paul at the Ford Parkway bridge.

***

Willows, cottonwoods, pin oaks and locusts line popular Lake Phalen in east St. Paul. A 3.2-mile trail loops around the lake, sticking close to the shoreline most of the way at Phalen Regional Park. From U.S. Hwy. 61 north of downtown St. Paul, go east onto Phalen Drive. Park in the lot for either the Phalen Lakeside Activity Center or the Phalen Beach House. The paved trail runs north-south immediately east of the lots.

Scott County

Hikers can head through a forest of yellow, orange and red

maple and olive-colored basswood at Spring Lake Regional Park. A 1.54-mile paved lollipop trail includes part of the Spring Lake Regional Trail. From Minn. Hwy. 13 in Prior Lake, take Eagle Creek Avenue NE northwest. Turn left/west onto 154th Street then left/south onto Stemmer Ridge Road, and lastly left/southeast onto Skuya Drive NW into the park. Use the lot on the road's left/north side and take the path east then south on the regional trail.

***

A canopy of maple and oak leaves awaits hikers at Murphy-Hanrehan Park Reserve. The 1.8-mile Knob Trail loops through the woodlands as well as past Hanrehan Lake and a pond. Watch for the hooded warbler; the park is the songbird's only known nesting site in Minnesota. From Minn. Hwy. 13 and Egan Drive on the Prior Lake-Savage border, take the latter east. Turn right/south onto County Road 27/Dakota Avenue then left/east onto 154th Street, and right/ south onto Murphy Lake Boulevard. Once in the park, take the first left/east and park. The trail leaves from the lot's southeast corner.

***

A wetlands may not seem like the best place to see fall colors, but often the uplands of such areas make for excellent autumn hikes. One such spot is the Louisville Swamp area of the Minnesota Valley National Wildlife Refuge. A 4.8-mile round trip hike on a segment of the State Corridor Trail – the trail includes part of the Little Prairie Loop and a connector trail – heads through large cottonwoods, ash, willows and maples along the Minnesota River. From Shakopee, take U.S. Hwy. 169 south. Exit right/west onto Red Rock Drive. Turn left/west onto 145th Street. The road ends at the parking lot for the trailhead. From the parking lot, take the Little Prairie Loop west, go north on the connector trail to the State Corridor Trail, then once at the trail go east. Turn back at the boundary for the Carver Rapids Unit, which is managed by the Minnesota DNR.

***

Yellow, orange and russet leaves in a farm setting make for a trip into autumns past at Cedar Lake Farm Regional Park. A 0.4-mile paved path circles through the wooded farmstead, passing a barn, corn cribs, and small beach along Cedar Lake. From New Prague, take Minn. Hwy. 19 east. Turn left/north onto County Road 89, right/east onto County Road 2, then left/north onto Juniper Avenue. A large lot for the park is on the right/east.

Washington County

Day hikers can explore wooded gorges that run near the Mississippi River in Cottage Grove Ravine Regional Park. Because of the varied hardwood trees – ash, aspen, birch and maple – the 2-mile packed turf Ravine Trail makes for a pretty autumn walk. From U.S. Hwy. 61 in Cottage Grove, go northeast on County Road 19 then right/southeast onto E. Point Douglas Road. The park service road is a left/northeast turn. Head to the second parking lot, located where the entry road loops back on itself, then walk northeast on the far-right trail.

***

Hikers can enjoy a walk through a woodlands and a on long pier at Big Marine Park Reserve. The unnamed trail in the Washington County park runs 0.75-miles round-trip. The turf trail leaves from the park's western side and enters a deciduous forest, which makes for a colorful walk among yellow, orange, red, russet and olive leaves in autumn. From Forest Lake, take Minn. Hwy. 97 east. Turn left/south onto County Road 15/Morning Trail North. The park entry road (aka Lomond Trail North) is on the left/east. When the entry road splits, go straight/west, following it to the last/northernmost parking lot (the road loops back onto itself at the lot).

***

A variety of autumn colors can be enjoyed in the maple-oak forests at Lake Elmo Park Reserve. The 3.8-mile Eagle Point Trail loops around the wooded lake for which the route is named. Paper birch, ash, and cottonwood, as well as several types of evergreens, dot the landscape. From Minn. Hwy. 36 in Lake Elmo, take County Road 17/Lake Elmo Road south. Turn right/west onto County Road 14/Stillwater Boulevard then left/south onto Keats Avenue and enter the reserve. After passing the Nordic Center, go right/west into a parking lot. The trail is on the lot's west side.

***

Day hikers can learn about the power of floods on the St. Croix River via the Riverside Trail at William O'Brien State Park. The 1.5-mile trail loops through a floodplain and typically is open during summer and autumn when water levels have gone down. The fresh scent of pine needles upon the trail and the gentle rush of water along the river's rock walls instantly lulls you into a feeling of serenity. Roughly half of the trail follows the river, mainly through a good mix of hardwoods common to a floodplain forest in this region. During autumn, their leaves turn gold, red, orange and brown. Across the water is Wisconsin, and with the two undeveloped shorelines, tranquility reigns. From Marine on St. Croix, take Minn. Hwy. 95 north into the park. Turn right/east onto O'Brien Trail North/County Road 33. The road curves south, dead ending in a parking area alongside Lake Alice. The trail begins at the picnic grounds immediately east of the parking lot.

***

Hikers can enjoy fall colors alongside a river and creek on

Brown's Creek State Trail. The 5.9-mile (one-way) trail connects Stillwater and the Gateway State Trail in Grant. A mile of the trail parallels the St. Croix River while another two miles sticks to its namesake creek. Leaves usually peak late September to mid October. From downtown Stillwater, take Minn. Hwy. 95 north. Park in either lot on the road's right/east before or after Laurel Street. The trailhead runs north from Laurel Street east of the lots.

Wright County

In an area where farm fields and now urbanization dots the landscape, there remains a spot that early French explorers called the Bois Grand – or as author Laura Ingalls Wilder later described it, the Big Woods – a vast continental forest of maple and basswood. In Lake Maria State Park, the 3.6-mile Big Woods Loop Trail loops through a remnant of the famed landscape that pioneers found when they arrived in Minnesota and Wisconsin. The fall colors usually peak in October, turning the canopy brilliant hues of yellow, orange and red. Bring a picnic lunch for the lake. From Monticello, take County Road 39 west. Turn right/north onto County Road 111 then enter the park by going left/west onto Park Road. After passing the park office, turn left/south onto the road leading to the Trail Center, where there is a parking lot and trailhead.

***

Fall foliage abounds along the North Fork Crow River at Humphrey Arends County Park. A 0.45-mile round trip mowed trail runs past a picnic area into the woods. From Buffalo, take County Road 12S south. Turn right/west onto County Road 107 then right/north onto County Road 9. The park entrance is on the left/west just before crossing the river. Public river access is offered for canoes.

South

Two geographic features define this region of Minnesota – the hilly Driftless Area along the Mississippi River and the flat Great Plains. Vastly different trees grow in these two predominantly rural areas, marking the transition between the Eastern forest and the continents' expansive plains. Look for maple and basswood in the Driftless Area and trees common to oak savannas in the prairies.

Riverview Trail

John A. Latsch State Park

A beautiful view of the Mississippi River resplendent in fall colors awaits each autumn at John A. Latsch State Park.

The 1-mile round trip Riverview Trail heads to the top of Mount Charity, a bluff alongside Ol' Man River. The trail consists of nearly 600 steps that climbs a deep ravine in the bluff.

To reach the trailhead, from Winona take U.S. Hwy. 61 north. In about 10 miles, turn left/southwest into the park. There's no entry fee, and the parking lot is wedged between the highway and the bluff. The trail heads south from the lot.

During the autumn, the bluffside brims with color: the yellows of birch, ironwood, black walnut, and elm; the oranges and scarlets of oaks; the golds, oranges and reds of maples; and the olive of basswood. Evergreen cedar accents the harvest hues.

Mount Charity is one of three rocky bluffs in the area that rise above 500 feet. During the 1850s, steamboat captains relied on them to navigate the Mississippi. They named the bluffs Faith, Hope and Charity.

In addition to being charitable with autumn colors, the bluff-land is rich in wildlife, some of which you'll be able to see now that summer's green foliage has thinned. Among the mammals are coyote, fox, opossum, squirrels, raccoons, and white-tailed deer. Peregrine falcons and bald eagles grace the skies, though you'll have the best chance of seeing them once you reach the blufftop.

In large part, the bluff was simply too steep for development, so was saved for the Driftless Area's wildlife. Thank park namesake John A. Latsch, a local businessman, for ensuring it was open to the public. In 1925, he purchased the bluff and persuaded an adjacent landowner to donate with him about 350 acres to the state for a park. Latsch was fairly familiar with the three bluffs, as he often fished the river below them. A few years later, he also donated land that became Perrot State Park, downriver in neighboring Wisconsin. The Minnesota park has since expanded and now totals 450 acres.

There are a couple of lookout points along the way where you can rest. The trail's steps rise does range from five inches to a foot, so be sure to watch where you place your feet.

At Mount Charity's top, hikers are treated to an impressive view of the river below, a blue ribbon through a landscape wrapped in gold leaves. Harvest hues fill the bluffsides on both sides of the river. Lock and Dam No. 5 can be seen to the southeast with barges lazily making their last trips of the season through it.

At this spot on the Mississippi, almost all of the floodplain sits on the Wisconsin side. Green ash, silver maple, and river birch dominate the sloughs and river valley. All turn similar hues of yellow in autumn.

Green ash is among the first trees to change colors in autumn, often the first week of September. A common ash species, it quickly takes over old fields and other disturbed sites. It

Autumn colors stretch across the horizon from the top of Mount Charity along the Mississippi River.

grows up to 82 feet high with a trunk diameter of up to 24 inches. Young green ash has smooth bark, but it becomes thick and fissured with age. A major concern for green ash is the emerald ash borer, an invasive species. Minnesota's green ash has no protection against it.

Silver maple is one of the most common trees in the United States but not found in the west-central part of Minnesota. Highly adaptable, it often can be spotted along waterways and in wetlands. The silver maple also is fast-growing; a 10-year-old sapling can stand up to 26 feet high, making it the best bet for future NFL lineman in the woods. It tops out, though, at 82 feet. It used to be a favorite in urban landscaping, but because its roots crack sidewalks and old pipes, and as it resprouts quickly, many cities now ban its planting.

River birch, also known as black birch or water birch, usually grows in floodplains and wetlands. It can reach a height of

100 feet. The base of the river birch usually consists of several slender trunks, each of which can grow up to 60 inches in diameter. The bark of young river birch consists of loose layers of curling scales and often looks as if it has been damaged, but that's not the case. As the tree matures, those scales form hard plates.

After taking in the views, return the way you came. A path does briefly lead away from the blufftop into the woods, but it quickly dissolves into a deer trail with little to see. If children are with you, make sure they stay away from the blufftop's edges.

Other South Trails

Big Stone County

Lakeshore cottonwood, ash, and silver maple make for a colorful autumn walk at Big Stone Lake State Park Bonanza Area. The 2-mile round trip Bonanza Area Hiking Club Trail mostly follows the shoreline of Big Stone Lake, the source of the Minnesota River. Away from the lake, the trail crosses part of an oak-basswood forest. From Ortonville, drive Minn. Hwy. 7 about 15 miles northwest. Turn left/west onto 320th Street. Upon entering the park, take the second left/west, which leads to the boat launch, and park in the lot. The trail heads northwest from the parking lot.

Blue Earth County

A nice urban trail to enjoy autumn leaves is the section of the Minnesota River Trail in Mankato. Try the 0.5-mile round trip segment that runs through Sibley Park. On sunny days, a variety of harvest hues reflect off the Minnesota River. Autumn colors peak late September to mid-October. Several other pathways at the park are lined with trees. From U.S. Hwy. 169 in

Mankato, exit onto South Riverfront Drive then take Owatonna Street north. Go left/west onto Sibley Parkway, which enters the park. Leave your vehicle in the second lot and cross the park road to the trail.

***

Autumn colors abound on the Red Jacket Trail running between Mankato and Rapidan. To stay in the woods, hike the 3.75-mile round trip segment from Huffy Lane north to the bridge over the LeSueur River. The bridge runs across former railroad tresses 80 feet above the water. Leaves usually peak between late September to mid October. From Mankato, take County Road 33 south. Turn right/west onto Huffy Lane. Park on the road shoulder at the trailhead.

Brown County

Red, orange and yellow maple trees and golden grasses await hikers at Flandrau State Park during fall. To enjoy both autumn leaves and prairie, try a combination of three trails. The Ridge Trail to the Grasslands Trail to the north side of the Bluebird Loop Trail to the eastern segment of the Bluebird Trail then back on the Ridge Trail covers 1.6-miles round trip. The maples also are fantastic at the park's picnic area. From the junction of U.S. Hwy. 14 and Minn. Hwys. 15/68 in New Ulm, take the latter southeast. Turn right/southwest onto Center Street then left/southeast onto Summit Avenue. Go right/southwest on County Road 26 and enter the park. Park in the lot next to the RV sanitation station and head northwest onto the Ridge Trail.

Chippewa County

Autumn colors abound alongside the Chippewa River at Lagoon Park in Montevideo. A 0.6-mile trail combined with the campsite road loops beside a wide meander in the river. From the junction of Minn. Hwy. 7/29 with Canton Avenue in Montevideo, take the latter east. Turn left/north onto North Parkway Avenue. After going under the highway, go left/west onto Forest Avenue. Leave your vehicle in the lot at the park's southwest corner.

Cottonwood County

Woodlands full of autumn leaves usually are hard to come by on the prairie. One place to locate them, however, is along rivers where trees can flourish. In Cottonwood County, Mayflower Park along the Des Moines River in Windom fits the bill. Follow the 1-mile round trip disc golf course trail through the woods. From County Road 17 in Windom, take Drake Avenue south. Turn left/east onto the dirt road and follow it the park's parking lot.

Dodge County

Finding autumn colors on the prairie can be difficult, but there are a number of small spots, such as the Iron Horse Prairie Scientific and Natural Area. The 2.9-mile round trip Iron Horse Trail follows the railroad grades of where two former spurs diverged. Various shrubs and trees have taken root along the former grades; meanwhile, the prairie grasses preserved there turn a beautiful gold color that stands out at sunset. From Hayfield, take Minn. Hwy. 56 south. Turn left/east onto County Road N. The natural area's entrance is on the right/south in a half-mile. Park on the road shoulder.

Faribault County

Finding woodlands with great autumn leaf displays in the prairie always is a challenge. Among the best places to look for such woodlands are lakes. Such a spot can be found at 20-acre Pihl's Park. There, a small woods with a nature trail borders a portion of Rice Lake with colors peaking in late September to early October. From Blue Earth, take Interstate 90 east. Exit right/south onto Minn. Hwy. 22. Go right-straight/south onto County Road 118. The park entry is on the right/west.

Fillmore County

A riverside resplendent with fall colors, a quaint small town, and 300-foot limestone bluffs await hikers on the Root River State Trail in Lanesboro. Fall colors usually peak early to mid-October on a 3.4-mile round trip segment of the trail. In Lanesboro, park near the Root River Trail Center on Milwaukee Road between Parkway and Kenilworth avenues. Take the trail southwest, turning back at the Grit Road crossing.

Freeborn County

Gold, red and orange maples and chartreuse-colored basswood leaves light up Myre-Big Island State Park in Albert Lea. The leaves usually reach their peak about mid-October on the looping 1.5-mile Big Island Trail. This trail circles the 120-acre wooded island in the middle of Albert Lea Lake. In Albert Lea, take County Road 46 east. Turn right/south onto County Road 38. Park in the lot when the road ends on Big Island.

Goodhue County

Yellow, orange and red maples with tan and russet oaks await hikers on Barn Bluff, a Red Wing icon. The 1.66-mile round trip South Trail heads through the wooded portion of the sandstone bluff and via the Kiwanis Stairway takes you to the top. The East Scenic Overlook offers a view of the surrounding river valley at 30 stories up. From U.S. Hwy. 61 in downtown Red Wing, go southeast onto Plum Street. Next, head left/northeast onto Fifth Street. When the road crosses under Hwy. 61, find a parking spot along the street. The trailhead is on the road's left/northwest side.

***

Hikers can traverse the top and base of a bluff looming 430 feet above Lake Pepin at Frontenac State Park. The 2.6-mile Bluff Side Loop Trail offers impressive views, as it heads up and down the steep bluff with a series of wooden stairs and switchbacks. Fall is a particularly good time to visit with the bird migration through the area at its peak and the leaves resplendent in an array of harvest colors. The trees change with the elevation; the trail at the top of the bluff is a mix of aspen, basswood, elm, maple and oak while cottonwood, maple and willow dominate the trail along the bluff's bottom. Fall colors usually peak in late September to mid-October. From the park entrance, go left/northwest on County Road 28; follow the road where it loops back upon itself and forms a parking lot.

***

A variety of trees and bushes light up Lake Byllesby Regional Park each autumn. Try the five stacked loop trails in the park's undeveloped northwest corner for the greatest range of leaf colors. On the 2.2-mile round trip hike are alder, red-osier dogwood, willow, sumac, and Amur maple. From Cannon Falls, take County Road 20/Fifth Street north. Turn left/west onto County Road 17, which becomes County Road 88 along the way, then left/south onto Harry Avenue and right/west onto Gerlach Way. The parking lot is on the right/north just before the Echo Point Road intersection.

Houston County

Among the most scenic hikes in Minnesota is the Root River

State Trail, and that's especially so in autumn. A range of fall colors line the trail, thanks to the great variety of trees that grow here. Riverside features black ash, willow, box elder, cottonwood and elm while the highlands boast maples, basswood and oaks. A great segment of the trail to hike begins in Houston and runs 2.3 miles west to a picnic area for a 4.6-mile round trip. From Minn. Hwy. 76 in Houston, turn north on Plum Street and park at the Houston Nature Center. The nature center as well as the International Owl Center just two blocks away are well worth a visit, and if you have little ones, they'll love the playground near the trailhead.

Jackson County

Oaks grace the ravines and river slopes at Kilen Woods State Park along the Des Moines River. To enjoy the autumn colors in an area dominated by farm fields, try the 1.1-mile round trip Rock Creek Trail to south on the Sioux Trail then the looping Riverside Trail. From Jackson, take County Road 14/10 west. Turn right/north onto County Road 17 then a right/east onto County Road 24. Park in the lot and look for the picnic shelter for the trailhead.

Lac Qui Parle County

A number of trees hug the shores of Boehnke Slough and the stream flowing into it at Kibler State Wildlife Management Area. You'll need to follow game trails or degraded footpaths through the wildlife area, which is home to deer and pheasant. Stay alongside the creek and slough shores for the best autumn colors. From Montevideo, take U.S. 212 west. Turn right/north onto U.S. Hwy. 75. In Bellingham, go left/west onto County Road 30. At the treeline west of 165th Avenue, park off the side of the road, and walk north into the wildlife area.

Le Sueur County

Day hikers can visit the classic Big Woods of old at Sakatah Lake State Park. The 2.4-miles round trip Oak Tree Trail and Big Woods Loop heads through a forest of basswood, oak and maple, all resplendent in harvest hues during fall. From Waterville, take Minn. Hwy. 60 east. Turn left/north at the park entrance. When the park road splits, go right/northeast. Park in the first lot. Hike the side of the road back, crossing the Sakatah Singing Hills State Trail. The Oak Tree Trail is the next junction; go right/west onto it. The trail leads to the Big Woods Loop.

Lincoln County

Each autumn, yellow and red leaves light up the white ash bordering the two lakes at Ash Lake State Wildlife Management Area. A 1.5-mile round trip jeep trail runs along North Ash Lake's west shore and then splits and traverses South Ash Lake's northern shore. While there, keep an eye out for white-tailed deer, pheasant, waterfowl, and doves. White ash usually is limited to southeastern Minnesota and is a rare find on the prairie. From Ivanhoe, take U.S. Hwy. 75 south. Turn right/west onto 260th Street. On North Ash Lake's western side, look for a jeep trail heading south. Park off the side of the road and walk the trail south.

Lyon County

In a prairie covered by farm fields, a woods sporting fall colors may seem like a dream, but such places exist, especially along riverways. The 1.3-mile round trip River Trail at Camden State Park is one such spot. Yellow-, orange- and red-leaved maples as well as golden basswood fill the Redwood River Valley here. From Marshall, take Minn. Hwy. 23 south. Turn right/west on County Road 68 then right/north on County Road 83.

Turn at the next left into a parking lot. The trail begins at the bridge crossing the river.

Martin County

Oak, basswood and several other hardwoods brighten the prairie in autumn colors at Cedar Creek Park in Fairmont. A 1.8-mile paved trail and a little more than 3 miles of mowed nature trails run through the park, which is almost entirely wooded. From Minn. Hwy. 15 in Fairmont, go west on County Road 20/Lake Aires Road then turn right/north onto Cedar Park Road; a parking lot is at the road's end with trails running either west or east from the lot's north side.

Mower County

Autumn leaves abound in the 518-acre hardwood forest at Jay C. Hormel Nature Center. The 1.8-mile combo of the Yellow and White trails with the connectors between them take you into the heart of the forest. In east Austin, take County Road 61 north. Turn right/east into the nature center. From the parking lot, take the connector southeast past the Rock to the looping Yellow Trail; a connector links the Yellow to the looping White Trail. The loops cross North Branch Dobbins Creek several times.

Murray County

Forests of oak, hackberry, basswood, elm and ash await at Lake Shetek State Park. The 0.8-mile round trip Picnic Trail is a great way to enjoy the forest's autumn colors as well as take in scenic views of Lake Shetek. From Slayton, drive U.S. Hwy 59 north. Turn left/southeast onto Minn. Hwy. 30 then in Currie go left/north onto County Road 38. Finally, turn left/northwest onto County Road 37 and enter the park. The road ends at a parking lot with the trail leaving from its southwest corner.

Nicollet County

Among the best spots in southwestern Minnesota to enjoy autumn colors is Seven Mile Creek County Park between St. Peter and North Mankato. The 2.3-mile looping Trail 8 (marked yellow on park maps) heads up and down the sides of wooded hills surrounding Seven Mile Creek. The park covers more than 600 acres, most of it forested. Leaves peak late September to mid October. From Mankato, take U.S. Hwy. 169 north. Turn left/west into the park. Follow the park road all the way to its end, where you can leave your vehicle in the Back Lot and locate the trailhead.

***

Though Fort Ridgely State Park is better known for its historic importance on the Plains in the U.S.-Dakota War of 1862, forests cover its ravines and hills, making it an ideal place to enjoy autumn leaves. Try the 1.8-mile round trip Valley Trail (sometimes referred to on maps and brochures as the Lower Valley Trail), which runs through a maple, basswood and ash woods overlooking Ft. Ridgely Creek. From St. Peter, take County Road 5/Old Fort Road west. Turn left/south onto Minn. Hwy. 4 then right/west onto County Road 21, and finally right/north onto County Road 30. Use the Main Camp and Creek Picnic Area parking lot.

Nobles County

The reflection of autumn trees in two lakes make for a beautiful fall hike at Maka-Oicu County Park. Narrow, degraded footpaths link West Graham and Jack lakes as well as run by a small stream connecting them. From Worthington, take U.S. Hwy. 59 north. Turn right/east onto 140th Street, which becomes Layfette Avenue when the road curves north; the avenue then naturally becomes Tripp Road. At the T-intersection when Tripp Road goes east, go left/west. The park entrance is on the left/west.

Olmsted County

Hikers can head through a large oak forest at Chester Woods Park. The 5.3-mile North Trail, Prairie Ridge, and Dam Overlook Loop overlooks tree-shrouded Bear Creek, runs alongside pretty Chester Lake, and passes prairie areas whose grasses turn gold in fall. From Rochester, take U.S. Hwy. 14 east. Turn right/south onto the park entry road; when the road splits, go right/west and park in the roundabout. The trail first crosses the prairie then enters the woods.

Pipestone County

Several impressive sights await hikers on a lone trail at Pipestone National Monument, particularly during autumn. The 0.75-mile Circle Trail heads through a woodlands of yellow-brown-leaved oak and crimson-, maroon- and bronze-colored white ash, past golden tallgrass prairie and red quartzite blocks and historic Native American quarries, and to the base of Winnewissa Falls. In Pipestone, drive north on U.S. Hwy 75. Turn left/west on County Road 67 and park in the lot where the road loops back on itself.

Redwood County

An oak woodland awaits hikers at Cedar Mountain Scientific and Natural Area. A 0.4-mile round trip trail passes boulders and leads to the woods, where autumn's gold leaves stand out against the large gray rocks, many draped in green moss. The woodlands is thin enough to walk through without a footpath.

From Redwood Falls, take Minn. Hwy. 19 west. Turn right/north onto County Road 17. At the natural area, park off the side of the road and walk east toward the rocks and woods.

Renville County

One stretch of the Minnesota River in the prairie that brims with harvest colors is River Warren Outcrops Scientific and Natural Area. A 1.6-mile trail loops through the woodlands. Bur oak covers the rock outcrops area above the river while silver maple, American elm, rock elm, and the rare (for Minnesota) Kentucky coffee tree rule the floodplain forest. From Redwood Falls, take County Road 101 north; upon crossing the Minnesota River, it becomes County Road 1. Turn left/northwest onto County Road 15. After passing County Road 21, watch for the natural area driveway and parking lot on the left/south.

Rice County

A picturesque waterfall awaits hikers at Nerstrand Big Woods State Park. The 1-mile round trip walk via Hidden Falls Trail is especially beautiful in autumn with yellow, orange, red sugar maple and amber ironwood, bronze-colored basswood, and russet-leaved oak lining the path. Hidden Falls sits in a glade amid this northern hardwoods forest, and boasts a 12-foot drop over a 90-foot wide ledge. From Faribault, take St. Paul Avenue/Cannon City Boulevard northeast. Turn right/east onto Nerstrand Boulevard, which becomes Kane Avenue when it curves north, then go left/west onto County Road 40. Take the first/north to the parking area; from there, walk east on the White Oak Trail to the Hidden Falls Trail.

***

Golden aspen and orange-yellow maple leaves await hikers at River Bend Nature Center in Faribault. One great option at the park is the 1.4-mile Owl and Trout Lily trails, which loop through a floodplain forest. Part of the trail runs alongside the Straight River. From First Street NW in Faribault, take Sixth Avenue SE south. Turn left/east onto Division Street East then right/south onto 10th Avenue SE, which when it curves east becomes Fifth Street SE. Next, turn right/south onto Rustad Road. Park at the lot for the interpretive center.

Rock County

Leaves aren't the only flora that changes color in autumn. Out on the prairie, the real show is the tallgrass. Among the best spots in Minnesota to see this is Blue Mounds State Park where a 1-mile round trip segment of the Upper Mound and Upper Cliffline trails offers a fantastic view from atop a 90-foot high quartzite outcropping. Looking west, bluestem grass turns a fiery red each autumn as buffalo graze in the distance. Perhaps the best day to visit is around 6:30 p.m. on the autumn equinox when a 1,250-foot long line of rocks, set in an east-west direction, lines up with the setting sun. From Luverne, take U.S. Hwy. 75 north. Turn right/east onto County Road 8 then the next left/north. Park in the lot at the road's end and head to Eagle Rock Vista and the trail.

Sibley County

A small upland woods brightens with autumn colors at Revanche Wildlife Management Area. You'll need to rely on game trails and degraded footpaths in the woods, but a jeep trail leads to the treeline. In addition to autumn leaves, watch for deer, turkey, pheasants and doves in the woods. From Glencoe, take U.S. Hwy. 212 east. Turn right/south on Minn. Hwy. 25; in Green Isle, the road goes left/east. A driveway for the wildlife area is on the right/south about 0.75 miles from the turn. Walk the jeep trail south to the woods.

Steele County

The glorious autumn colors of maple, oak and aspen can be enjoyed at Rice Lake State Park. The 2.4-mile Hiking Club Trail loops through several such woods and cross meadows featuring bur oak. About half of the trail runs alongside scenic Rice Lake. From Owatonna, take County Road 19/Rose Street east. Turn right/south onto County Road 40 into the park. When the park road splits, go left/southeast and follow it the parking lot at the walk-in and group campsites; follow the turf trail to the trail shelter.

Swift County

Hikers can enjoy the fall colors of oak, ash and basswood as well as sparkling lakes at Monson Lake State Park. The wooded 2-mile round trip Hiking Club Trail passes Monson and West Sunberg lakes, where migrating waterfowl stop over during autumn. From Benson, take Minn. Hwy. 9 east. Turn right/south onto 160th Avenue NE, which when it swerves left/east becomes 15th Street NE. The park entry is on the left/north with the road ending at a parking lot. The trailhead is at the lot's southeast corner.

Traverse County

A small grove of hardwoods brightens the prairie in autumn colors at Robin Hood Waterfowl Production Area. A 0.33-mile round trip farm road can be hiked to the treeline and then extended by using game trails or degraded footpaths. During autumn, expect to see migrating birds flying about the ponds around the grove. From Elbow Lake, take Minn. Hwy. 54 south. Turn right/west onto Minn. Hwy. 27. In Wheaton, go left/south onto U.S. Hwy. 75, then right/south onto County Road 9, right/west onto County Road 4, and left/south onto County Road 55. Take the next left/east and look for a driveway to the farm road on the right/south. Park in the driveway and walk south.

Wabasha County

One of the best urban areas in the Midwest to enjoy fall colors is the small town of Wabasha. For seven weeks from September through October, the small town celebrates a harvest festival. You can enjoy the festivities and take a nice stroll on the 0.8-mile round trip riverwalk. The Wisconsin shoreline on the opposite side of the Mississippi River is lit up in golden hues, the perfect match to the streets' autumn decorations. To reach the riverwalk, park in downtown Wabasha. Finding a spot on Big Jo Alley near Pembroke Avenue is best, as the National Eagle Center is at the corner of those two streets. The riverwalk is behind the center.

Waseca County

Walkers can enjoy autumn leaves along pathways at Northwest Nature Park. About 0.75 miles of hiking trails run through the park in three small loops. From downtown Waseca, take Minn. Hwy. 13 north. Turn left/west onto 13th Avenue NW and then left/south onto 12th Avenue NW. Upon arriving at Northwest Park, leave your vehicle parked against the curb and walk west past the playground. At the trail junction, go right/northwest. The loops begin in 0.13 miles on the trail's west side.

Watonwan County

Hikers can enjoy autumn leaves reflected in a pretty lake at Wood Lake Wildlife Management Area. While wetlands make circling Wood Lake difficult at best, you can walk about 100 feet one-way from the parking area to the lake and then its northwest shore for as far as game trails and degraded footpaths will take you. From St. James, take Minn. Hwy. 4 north. Turn left/west onto Minn. Hwy. 30, right/north onto County Road 18, and left/west onto T-212. Look for the entrance to the wildlife area on the left/south just before the road curves northwest.

Winona County

A great view of the Mississippi River awaits at the Great River Bluffs State Park on the 2.2-mile round trip Kings Bluff Trail. After heading through a forest of white pine and the yellow to maroon-colored leaves of ash trees, the trail arrives at Kings Bluff, which offers a spectacular vista of the Mississippi River valley, a blue ribbon surrounded by the yellows of various birch and aspen. From Interstate 90 near the Minnesota-Wisconsin border, take County Road 3 north. Turn right/east onto Kipp Drive, which becomes Park Road. About two miles in, look for a small parking lot on the left/northwest. The trail heads northwest from the lot.

***

Hikers can head through and below a maple and oak forest at Whitewater State Park. The 4.5-mile round trip Dakota Trail crosses the ridge above the Whitewater River, where you walk beneath the harvest-hued canopy, then descends to the waterway for a great view of the gold, orange, scarlet and tan trees covering the hill. From Winona, take U.S. Hwy. 14 west. In St. Charles, turn right/north onto Minn. Hwy. 74. Use the Nature Store parking lot.

Yellow Medicine County

Hikers can head through an oak savanna on their way to

Fall colors run from the blufftops to the Mississippi River at Great River Bluffs State Park. Photo courtesy of Minnesota DNR.

outcrops of 2.65 billion-year-old rock at Swedes Forest Scientific and Natural Area. A 2.1-mile round trip jeep trail runs through the natural area. Twenty-four other kinds of trees and shrubs can be seen there as well, making for great fall colors in the prairie. From Redwood Falls, take Minn. Hwy. 19 west then turn right/north onto County Road 7. Go left/west onto 440th Street, which becomes 208th Avenue. Use the second driveway into the natural area, which has a gate on the trail, and park along the road.

The sugar maple dominates neighboring Wisconsin's forests, delivering impressive autumn colors.

On the Border

The fall colors don't stop at the state line. If living in a border county or traveling near Wisconsin, Iowa or the Dakotas, you may want to check out some of the great autumn trails "over there." Wisconsin's trails largely are in the Driftless Area along the southeast border and classic Northwoods country along the northeast border. Iowa's trails sit in the Driftless Area in one county but are on the Great Plains for the rest of the southern border. Ditto with South and North Dakota, which form the state's western border. All of these areas sport rich tree communities – albeit isolated in the prairie – and include a few species rarely seen in Minnesota.

Wisconsin

Buffalo County

Day hikers can see ancient fossils on a spectacular vista that one time sat at the bottom of the sea. The 0.22-miles round trip Buena Vista Overlook Trail marks a must-see for anyone traveling the Wisconsin side of the Mississippi River. Located in Alma's Buena Vista County Park, it's an easy walk and a spectacular one in autumn. From the vista, a rainbow of leaf colors lead downhill to large swaths of gold around the Mississippi River. In Alma on Wis. Hwy. 35, turn east onto County Road E; known as North Street in town, it curves and becomes Second Street then curls again as ascending the bluff. Near the top, turn left/north onto Buena Vista Road. The road dead ends at the park entrance.

Burnett County

Day hikers can walk across an old railroad bridge over the St. Croix River at the St. Croix National Scenic Riverway and St. Croix State Forest on the Wisconsin-Minnesota border. The Gandy Dancer Trail, which starts dozens of miles south of the state forest in Polk County, at Danbury crosses the border into Minnesota. The trestle bridge segment is about two miles round trip. You'll head through a forested area. The mix of trees near the riverfront yields a fantastic multi-colored leaf display in autumn. An added bonus for autumn hikers: You'll probably spot a number of migrating waterfowl, including sandhill cranes. Also watch for bald eagles, osprey, northern harriers and hawks, all of which reside year-round in the area. In Danbury, parking for the trailhead is next to the walking route north of Wis. Hwy. 77 between and Wis. Hwy. 35 and North Glass Street. From the lot, take the trail north.

Douglas County

A walk along a pristine sand beach awaits day hikers of the Lake Superior shoreline in Bear Beach State Natural Area. The unmarked trail runs for up to 3.4-miles round trip along narrow Bear Beach. Hiking the shore, you'll get a good sense of what this area of the world looked like before Euro-Americans settled it. A thick woods hugs the sand's southern side while the lake stretches wide beyond to the north. Though the forest this far north is heavy on the evergreens – especially balsam fir, white pine and white spruce – in autumn the yellowed-colored leaves of paper birch and trembling aspen and the spring green of speckled alder are well-represented. From Brule, take U.S. Hwy. 2 west. In Maple, turn north onto County Road F. Next, go left/west onto Wis. Hwy. 13 then right/north onto Beck's Road. Park in the dirt lot at the end of Beck's Road near the Lake Superior shore.

***

A boreal forest may not seem like the best place to enjoy autumn leaves. The Superior Municipal Forest, however, delivers, with its extensive growth of gold-leafed white birch and aspen amid evergreen white and red pine, balsam, cedar, and black spruce. A 1.6-mile segment of the Millennium Trail winds through the woods. In Superior, at the 28th Street and Wyoming Avenue intersection, turn south to the municipal parking lot. The trail goes both east and west; skip the eastern side, which leads to multiple railroad tracks in Superior's industrial section.

La Crosse County

Hikers can walk alongside and cross a stream via five different bridges on the Halfway Creek Trail. The 3.4-mile trail connects Holmen to the Great River State Trail in Midway. Maple, aspen, oak and the occasional pine line the creek, making for a colorful autumn walk. Start at Halfway Creek Park in Holmen; the trailhead is on the park's southwest side. One good turn-around spot to avoid crossing under U.S. Hwy. 53 is the connector trail to Judith Court for a 1.13-mile round trip and three bridge crossings.

***

Autumn colors and great views await in the Greens Coulee-Savanna Oaks site in Onalaska. The Mississippi River Valley Conservancy's 81 acres includes a scenic bluff that rises 400 feet above the valley floor adjacent to the city's Greens Coulee Park. A 1.4-mile round trip trail heads to the bluff's peak, where reds, oranges and yellows fill much of the fall canopy along the way. From the intersection of U.S. Hwy. 53 and East Main Street in Onalaska, take the latter east. Turn left/northeast onto Green Coulee Road then right onto Clifford Drive. Look for the kiosk at the of the cul-de-sac, where parking is available.

Pepin County

Day hikers can explore a bluff steeped in majestic white oaks and legend high above Lake Pepin. The Maiden Rock Bluff Trail runs 1.4-miles round trip. It's located in the Maiden Rock State Natural Area, which preserves a blufftop prairie that turns golden in autumn. Beyond the giant oaks, sunlight sparkles off the blue lake, as if diamonds had been tossed across a turquoise cloth. From Stockholm, take County Road J north. Turn left/northwest onto County Road E then go left/west into Long Lane. The road dead ends at a grassy parking lot on the bluff-top. A trailhead is a few yards east of the lot and heads north from the road.

***

Day hikers can enjoy a walk alongside a lake and through the woods on the Silver Birch Park Trail. The 0.6-mile round trip trail runs through Silver Birch Park to Holden Park Campground. As if it were a mirror, Silver Birch Lake impressively reflects the blue sky and clouds on days when the wind is low. The reflection seems to stretch forever – that's not surprising as the lake's surface area covers 145 acres. A tree canopy covers the walking path, which makes for a nice autumn stroll when leaves change color. From Durand, head west on Wis. Hwy. 25 then turn left/south onto County Road P. Go left/south onto Silver Birch Road. At County Road NN/Round Hill Road, turn right/west. The next left/south is the park entry road.

Pierce County

Hikers can walk through a rare old growth oak forest on the Purple Trail at Kinnickinnic State Park. The 1.2-mile loop sits near the confluence of the St. Croix and Kinnickinnic rivers. Pioneers and 19th century logging companies cut most of the trees in this part of Wisconsin, but the trail passes through one of the few woodlands to escape the ax. The oaks are majestic, especially in autumn when their leaves turn tan, orange and brown. The trail includes a deck overlooking the confluence where eagles can be spotted. From Prescott, take Wis. Hwy. 29 east then turn left/north County Road F north. Turn left/west onto 820th Avenue then left/south into the park; follow the entry road west all of the way to its end and park in the St. Croix Picnic Area Lot.

***

Amber, orange and crimson leaves surround and reflect off of the blue waters at Nugget Lake County Park east of Ellsworth. The Nook Trail and the Lake Overlook combine for a mile-long round trip that gets you up close to 117-acre Nugget

Lake and to a great vista of it. The trees here are the same kind as those that made up the famous Big Woods of pioneer days. From Ellsworth, take U.S. Hwy. 10 east. Turn left/north onto County Road CC then right/east onto County Road HH, which curves south. The park entry is on the road's right/west side. Park in the lot where the road runs out.

Polk County

Fantastic river views beneath a colorful forest canopy await hikers on a pair of trails near Osceola. The Ridgeview Trail actually is two loops that only locals really know about. They run through the St. Croix National Scenic Riverway and the Osceola State Fish Hatchery on a bluff overlooking a St. Croix River back channel. The oranges and reds of maples dominate with the occasional pine grove. From Osceola, take Wis. Hwy. 35 north and turn left/north onto County Road S. The two trailheads are on the road's left/west side. Both trailheads have their own parking areas off of the road. Just beyond 93rd Avenue is the southernmost parking area, which is an excellent trailhead for either loop.

***

The splendor of fall colors combines with a vista of the St. Croix River and fascinating rock formations on the Summit Rock Trail at Interstate State Park. The 1-mile round trip trail heads to a bluff's highest point. Moss and autumn leaves cover the surrounding rock and ground while maples, basswood and eastern white pines line the trail. At the top, prickly pear cactus can be spotted amid the outcroppings. The highlight of the hike without question is the incredible view of the riverway from the summit. Looking north, the Old Man of the Dalles rock formation is visible. From St. Croix Falls, take Wis. Hwy. 35 south. Turn right/west into the park and follow the entry road to the parking lot across from the Lake O' the Dalles.

St. Croix County

Tucked within Wisconsin's dairy country is a hilly, wooded region that gives day hikers the chance to get back to nature. Glen Hills County Park offers a plethora of trails amid 700 acres of maple and oak trees. The 2-mile round trip Glen Lake East Trail goes downhill to a campground. Before hitting the trail, though, head to a scenic overlook of Glen Lake, ringed by red pines and hardwoods. From U.S. Hwy. 12 in Wilson, take County Road W north. Turn left/north onto Rustic Road 4 then go left/northwest onto Thompson Lane, which dead ends at the parking lot.

Trempealeau County

Great views of the Mississippi River await at Perrot State Park. The 2.4-mile round trip Brady's Bluff West and East trails are particularly impressive in autumn. Start up Brady's Bluff West Trail and pause at the hill's summit, which offers impressive views of the Mississippi River Valley, a brilliant blue ribbon through a forest of golden leaves. Descending the summit via the Brady's Bluff East Trail heads through a woods of russet-leaved oaks. From Wis. Hwy. 35 in Trempealeau, take 10th Street west. Turn right/north onto Park Road, which becomes South Park Road. Park in the lot before the boat launch; the trailhead is on the opposite side of the road.

Vernon County

Hikers can step back in time and walk through the woods as in the days of old at Wildcat Mountain State Park. The rugged 2.5-mile Old Settlers' Trail includes 390-feet of elevation change as heading through a forest of sugar maple, basswood and oak, all very colorful in autumn. An additional 0.8-mile round trip spur goes to the Taylor Hollow Overlook, which offers a fantastic view of the village of Ontario in the coulee below. From Westby, take Wis. Hwy. 27 north. In Cashton, turn right/east onto Wis. Hwy. 33. Once in the park, go left/east past the park office and at the split turn left/northwest to the Upper Picnic Area. Park there; a connector trail goes north to the Old Settlers' Trail.

Iowa

Allamakee County

Iowa's best fall color trails sit high on an ancient site over the Mississippi River. One of them, the 2-mile round trip Fire Point Trail at Effigy Mounds National Monument, passes Eagle Rock with a vista 300 feet above the river. Amber, pumpkin orange and scarlet leaves of sugar maple and bronze-colored basswood dominate the trail's northern slopes while the warmer southern side is lit with the russet of red oak, tan and brown of shagbark hickory, and the gold to burgundy of white ash. Hike during the early morning when mist rises off the river as high as the bluff, and there's little wonder why the Native American found these bluffs a spiritual place. From U.S. Hwy. 18 in Marquette, take Iowa Hwy. 76 north. Park at the visitor center.

***

Hikers can see up and down the Mississippi River valley in its full autumn glory at Mt. Hosmer Park. A 0.3-mile trail rings the top of the 450-foot high bluff with views of up to 50 miles away. Additional trails wind up and down the bluff's side. During autumn, the river valley will be decked out in an array of yellow leaves. From Iowa Hwy. 9 in Lansing, take North Sixth

Street north to the bluff's top.

***

The Driftless Area's famous autumn colors can be enjoyed at French Creek Wildlife Management Area. A 3.75-mile round trip jeep trail runs alongside winding French Creek, as tree-covered hills rise around you. From Waukon, take Iowa County 9 northeast. Turn left/north onto French Creek Road. The jeep trail is on the road's left/north side just before French Creek; park off the jeep trail and walk north.

Dickinson County

Autumn leaves abound at Gull Point State Park, nestled on the shores of West Okoboji Lake. The 1.5-mile Barney Peterson Nature Trail loops through a hardwoods forest. From Spirit Lake, take Iowa Hwy. 9 west. Turn left/south onto County Road 86 then left/east onto Edgewood Drive, which naturally becomes Harpen Street. Watch for the trailhead parking lot on the street's left/west side.

Emmet County

Hikers can enjoy fall foliage on the shores of a lake at tiny Okamanpeedan State Park. Located on the Minnesota-Iowa border, you'll need to rely on degraded footpaths to traverse the woods. From Fairmont, take Minn. Hwy. 15 south. In Iowa, turn right/west onto Hwy. A17 then right/north onto 510th Avenue (which naturally becomes 110th Street). Turn right/north onto a gravel road into the park.

Howard County

Fall foliage surrounds a beautiful lake at Lake Hendricks Park. The 2.3-mile Loop 2 circles the lake, staying in the woods the entire way. A portion of the trail runs alongside lovely Watson Creek. From Austin, take Interstate 90 east then exit south onto Minn. Hwy. 56. In LeRoy, turn right/south onto 775th Avenue, which at the Iowa border becomes Dale Avenue. Go right/west on Iowa Hwy. 9 and in Riceville turn right/north onto Hwy. T68/Addison Avenue then right/east into the park. Leave your vehicle in the lot north of the Lower Campground.

***

A small woodlands offers a bounty of autumn colors at the Miller Access Area. Degraded footpaths and game trails run through the site, which sits on an oxbow in the Upper Iowa River. From Spring Valley, take U.S. Hwy. 63 south. Before reaching Lime Springs, turn left/east onto 40th Street. Go left/north on Hwy. V36/Oak Avenue. After crossing the river, turn right/east at the first road and then a right/south on the frontage road. Take the next driveway left/east to a tiny parking lot.

Kossuth County

Autumn leaves light up a small forest on the southwest corner of a lake at Burt Lake Campground and Wildlife Area. A short mowed grass trail runs near Swag Lake, which is split by the Minnesota-Iowa border. From Fairmont, take Minn. Hwy. 15 south into Iowa. Turn left/east onto Hwy. A16 then left/north onto 40th Avenue. When the road splits, continue left-straight/north into the park.

Lyon County

Fall colors can be enjoyed along the scenic Rock River at Island Park. A half-mile segment of the Rock Rapids Bike Trail can be walked through a small woods and along the riverfront. A bridge crosses the river, offering pretty views of the shoreline dressed in harvest hues. From Luverne, take U.S. Hwy. 75 south. In Rock Rapids, go left-straight/east onto Iowa Hwy. 9

then turn left/north onto North Boone Street, which becomes Park Street and enters the park.

Mitchell County

Fall colors await along a bend in the Cedar River at Otranto Park. A short footpath runs beneath an orange and yellow canopy at the 5-acre park. From Austin, take U.S. Hwy. 218 south. Turn right/west onto Hwy. A19. The park's entry is on the right/north just before the Cedar River.

Osceola County

Autumn leaves along the Ocheyedan River can be seen at the Keller Wildlife Area. A 2.7-mile round trip jeep trail follows the river's western shore. The trail starts in the Ocheyedan Well Wildlife Area, which is prairie, and then a quarter of the way through enters the Keller Wildlife Area, where trees can be found. From Worthington, take U.S. Hwy. 59 south. Turn left/east onto Iowa Hwy. A22. After passing Hwy. L54, park off the road just before the river. Walk south on the river's west bank.

Winnebago County

Autumn colors can be enjoyed in the woods surrounding a pretty lake at small Rice Lake State Park. You'll have to rely on game trails and degraded footpaths to cross the forest. Colors usually peak in early October. From Albert Lea, take U.S. Hwy. 69 south to Lake Mills. On Main Street, turn left/east then go right/south onto 225th Avenue. Go left/east onto 425th Street then left/north onto 235th Avenue into the park. Follow paths into the woods east of 235th Avenue.

Winneshiek County

Orange, yellow and red leaves frame tall, white limestone

formations above the Upper Iowa River at Chimney Rock County Park. No formal trails run through the park, but intrepid explorers have carved out degraded footpaths in the woods above the river's west shore. From Decorah, take Hwy. A34/ Pole Line Road northwest. Turn right/north onto Hwy. W20/ Bluffton Road then left/west onto Chimney Rock Road. Park in the Chimney Rock Canoe Access lot on the road's right/ north side. Cross the road and head south.

Worth County

Autumn leaves fill tiny Ochee Yahola County Park. A 0.95-mile round trip jeep trail runs along the park's east side; the trail can be extended by walking on degraded footpaths and jeep trails winding through the woods. From Albert Lea, take U.S. Hwy. 65 south. Turn right/west onto County Road 1. At the state line, go left/east onto Iowa Hwy. 1 then right/west onto 495th Street. Park off the side of the road at the first jeep trail on the road's right/north side. Walk the jeep trail north to the end of the woodline.

South Dakota

Brookings County

Hikers can enjoy fall colors along beautiful Lake Tetonkaha at Oakwood Lakes State Park. The 1-mile (one-way) Mortimer Shoreline Trail follows the wooded eastern side of the lake. A historic cabin sits off the trail. From Brookings, take Interstate 29 north. Exit and go west on S.D. Hwy. 30 then turn right/ north onto Oakwood Shoreline Drive. Upon entering the park, turn left/west to the campground area. Follow the park road straight to a parking lot overlooking the lake and alongside the trail.

Deuel County

Autumn colors often are difficult to find on the prairie, but riverways and large lakes usually are good places to look. One such place is School Lake, located in Round Lake State Wildlife Management Area, where trees line the north and western shores. A degraded footpath runs about 3-miles round trip along half of the lake. From Milbank, take U.S. Hwy. 12 west. Turn left/south onto County Road 19, which upon entering Deuel County becomes County Road 443. Go right/west onto County Road 289; when the road splits, go left/south. Turn left/east onto 168th Street. As the road curves north, turn right/south onto a road leading into the wildlife area.

***

Autumn colors reflect off pretty Clear Lake at small Ulen Park. A short nature trail runs through the park. It's also a great spot to enjoy a picnic. From the city of Clear Lake, take S.D. Hwy. 22 east. Turn left/north onto Memorial Drive. Park near the fishing pier.

Minnehaha County

Great views of autumn leaves in a river valley await at Big Sioux State Recreation Area. The 1.2-mile round trip Valley of the Giants Trail sits on a bluff overlooking a wooded oxbow of the Big Sioux River. From Holly Boulevard and South Sioux Boulevard in Brandon, take the latter south. Turn right/west onto West Park Street then right/north onto the park. Leave your vehicle at the farthest north parking lot.

***

Fall foliage frames fascinating rock formations above Split Rock Creek at Palisades State Park. The 1.4-mile round trip South Wall Trail runs along the bluff overlooking the creek then crosses the stream via a historic century-old iron bridge.

Balancing, Chimney, King and Queen rocks can be seen along the way. From Garretson, take S.D. Hwy. 11 southwest. Turn right/south onto 485th Street then a right/west onto 255th Street into the park. When the park road curves north, turn left/west and park in the first lot on the right.

***

Autumn colors abound on the bluffs overlooking the Big Sioux River at Good Earth State Park. The 1.6-mile round trip River View Loop – which includes segments of the Vista Loop and River Trail – heads through woods much of the way and circles a savanna on the blufftop. From Sioux Falls, take S.D. 115 south. Turn left/east onto West 69th Street then right/south onto 480th Street/County Road 135. Go right/east into the park and leave your vehicle at the visitor center. From there, take the Vista Loop south to the River Trail and follow that southeast to the lollipop River View Loop.

***

Trees in all their autumn glory can be enjoyed along the scenic Big Sioux River via the Sioux Falls Bike Trail Loop. The entire trail makes a 19.1-mile circle of the city, but perhaps the best segment to enjoy fall colors is a 3.4-mile one-way segment from Yankton Trails Park east to Spencer Park. In Sioux Falls, from the junction of Interstate 229 and South Western Avenue, take the latter south. Turn left/west onto West 57th Street then left/north onto Park Access Road. After crossing the bridge, go left/east into Yankton Trails Park. A parking lot is on the right/north.

Moody County

Harvest-hued trees can be seen along the Big Sioux River at Flandreau Park. The short Oxbow Wetlands Nature Trail offers a great experience. From downtown Flandreau, take County

Road D east. Turn left/north on Flandreau Park Road.

Roberts County

A native woodland can be enjoyed on the shores of a historic lake at Hartford Beach State Park. The 0.75-mile round trip Campground to Beach Trail heads through the woods on the shores of Big Stone Lake. The park contains a prehistoric village, burial mounds, fur trapper cabin, and trading post, which can be reached via other forested trails. From Sisseton, take S.D. Hwy. 10 east. Turn right/south onto Interstate 29. Exit and go east onto S.D. Hwy. 15. Go left/north onto Hartford Beach Road and enter the park. When the park road splits, go left/northwest and park in the lot for the beach.

North Dakota

Cass County

Autumn colors line the Red River of the North on a trail that traverses several Fargo parks. The 4.9-mile (one-way) Red River Trail connects Lindenwood Park to Dike East Park. In Fargo from the junction of South University Drive and 17th Avenue, take the latter west. Turn right/south onto Roger Maris Drive. Park at the playground and take the walkway heading northeast to the trailhead.

***

Autumn leaves line the shores of the Sheyenne River in small Armour Park. Degraded footpaths follow the river, or you can stay on the mowed grass and follow the west side of the treeline as it curves around the river. From Interstate 94 and Sheyenne Street in West Fargo, take the latter north. Turn left/west onto U.S. Hwy. 10/Main Avenue, then right/north onto Ninth Street NW/County Road 19, and finally right/east onto Second Avenue NW, which ends at the park.

***

A small woodland sits on the south side of a wetlands at Magnolia State Game Management Area. No formal trails run through the 97-acre site, so be prepared for some "back-country" hiking, though in the woods degraded footpaths can be found. From Casselton, take Interstate 94 west. Exit and head north onto 145th Avenue SE. About 0.2 miles south of the railroad tracks, park off the side of the road and walk north-west into the woods.

Grand Forks County

Fall colors abound at heavily wooded Turtle River State Park. The 2.55-mile round trip Hollow River Trail runs along-side Turtle River. From Grand Forks, take U.S. Hwy. 2 west. Turn right/north onto Park Avenue Northeast. Go right/north onto Forest Street Northeast and after crossing the river look for a parking lot on the road's right/north side. Walk back across the bridge and use the trailhead on the road's right/west side.

***

A great place to see autumn leaves in Grand Forks is the Greenway, a 2,200-acre band of natural open space in the city and East Grand Forks. A walking path runs through the Green-way along the Red River. Try the 5.3-mile round trip segment of the walkway from the Demers Avenue bridge to the Grand Forks County Historical Society museum. Leave your vehicle at a parking space northwest of Demers Avenue just before cross-ing the bridge into Minnesota then walk south.

Pembina County

A lowland woodland of American elm, basswood and ironwood awaits hikers at Gunlogson State Nature Preserve near Icelandic State Park. Try the Basswood Trail, which runs 1.14-miles round trip when combined with the connector trails to the Wildwood Trail. From Cavalier, take N.D. Hwy. 5. Turn right/north into the park. After the entrance station, go right/north to the parking area and walk northeast across the green to the trailhead.

***

A lush wooded hillside that turns orange and yellow each autumn awaits at Tetrault Woods State Forest. A 4-mile round trip trail parallels the meandering Pembina River and two oxbows it has formed. From Walhalla, go south on N.D. Hwy. 32. The state forest entrance is on the right/west. A trail heads from the parking area over a wetlands then into higher, wooded country.

Richland County

If with kids, a nice place to enjoy autumn leaves is Chahinkapa Park. A paved walking path runs about 2-miles round-trip along the tree-lined Red River. A bonus is the Chahinkapa Zoo on the route, which adds about a quarter-mile to the walk. From Dakota Avenue in Wahpeton, go north on First Street. In one block, turn right/east onto Second Avenue. A parking lot is at the end of the road on the left/north with the walking path heading east.

Traill County

Fall colors light up a small bend in the Red River at tiny Belmont Park. A half-mile road runs through the campground with a spur to the river shore. From Mayville, take N.D. Hwy. 200 east. Turn left/north onto County Hwy. 81, then right/east onto County Hwy. 17, and finally left/north onto County Hwy.

2. At the Frog Point Monument, go right/east into the park. Leave your vehicle at the campground building and walk the road.

***

Hikers can enjoy fall colors on a bend in the Goose River at Woodland Park. Walk the park's perimeter alongside the river for a 0.75-mile hike. From N.D. Hwy. 200/First Street NE in Hillsboro, take Caledonia Avenue east. Turn left/north onto Third Street NE and park at the swimming pool.

Walsh County

Day hikers can walk through a woods alongside the Park River at the City of Grafton Walking Path and Trails. The Yellow Trail ("Trail 1" on some city maps) runs 1-mile round trip. From U.S. Hwy. 81 in Grafton, take West Fifth Street west. After McHugh Avenue, turn right/north onto the entry road for Leistikow Park. Park in the lot north of the campground and walk the trail north into the woods.

Bonus Section: Day Hiking Primer

You'll get more out of a day hike if you research it and plan ahead. It's not enough to just pull over to the side of the road and hit a trail that you've never been on and have no idea where it goes. In fact, doing so invites disaster.

Instead, you should preselect a trail (This book's trail descriptions can help you do that). You'll also want to ensure that you have the proper clothing, equipment, navigational tools, first-aid kit, food and water. Knowing the rules of the trail and potential dangers along the way also are helpful. In this special section, we'll look at each of these topics to ensure you're fully prepared.

Selecting a Trail

For your first few hikes, stick to short, well-known trails where you're likely to encounter others. Once you get a feel for hiking, your abilities, and your interests, expand to longer and more remote trails.

Always check to see what the weather will be like on the trail you plan to hike. While an adult might be able to withstand wind and a sprinkle here or there, for kids it can be pure misery. Dry, pleasantly warm days with limited wind always are best when hiking with children.

Don't choose a trail that is any longer than the least fit person in your group can hike. Adults in good shape can go 8-

12 miles a day; for kids, it's much less. There's no magical number.

When planning the hike, try to find a trail with a mid-point payoff – that is something you and definitely any children will find exciting about half-way through the hike. This will help keep up everyone's energy and enthusiasm during the journey.

If you have children in your hiking party, consider a couple of additional points when selecting a trail.

Until children enter their late teens, they need to stick to trails rather than going off-trail hiking, which is known as bushwhacking. Children too easily can get lost when off trail. They also can easily get scratched and cut up or stumble across poisonous plants and dangerous animals.

Generally, kids will prefer a circular route to one that requires hiking back the way you came. The return trip often feels anti-climatic, but you can overcome that by mentioning features that all of you might want to take a closer look at.

Once you select a trail, it's time to plan for your day hike. Doing so will save you a lot of grief – and potentially prevent an emergency. You are, after all, entering the wilds, a place where help may not be readily available.

When planning your hike, follow these steps:

• Print a road map showing how to reach the parking lot near the trailhead. Outline the route with a transparent yellow highlighter and write out the directions.

• Print a satellite photo of the parking area and the trailhead. Mark the trailhead on the photo.

• Print a topo map of the trail. Outline the trail with the yellow highlighter. Note interesting features you want to see along the trail and the destination.

• If carrying GPS, program this information into your device.

• Make a timeline for your trip, listing: when you will leave home; when you will arrive at the trailhead; your turn back time; when you will return for home in your vehicle; and when you will arrive at your home.

• Estimate how much water and food you will need to bring based on the amount of time you plan to spend on the trail and in your vehicle. You'll need at least two pints of water per person for every hour on the trail.

• Fill out two copies of a hiker's safety form. Leave one in your vehicle.

• Share all of this information with a responsible person remaining in civilization, leaving a hiker's safety form with them. If they do not hear from you within an hour of when you plan to leave the trail in your vehicle, they should contact authorities to report you as possibly lost.

Clothing

Footwear

If your feet hurt, the hike is over, so getting the right footwear is worth the time. Making sure the footwear fits before hitting the trail also is a good idea. With children, if you've gone a few weeks without hiking, that's plenty of time for feet to grow, and they may have just outgrown their hiking boots. Check out everyone's footwear a few days before heading out on the hike. If it doesn't fit, replace it.

For flat, smooth, dry trails, sneakers and cross-trainers are fine, but if you really want to head onto less traveled roads or tackle areas that aren't typically dry, you'll need hiking boots. Once you start doing any rocky or steep trails – and remember that a trail you consider moderately steep needs to be only half that angle for a child to consider it extremely steep – you'll want hiking boots, which offer rugged tread perfect for handling rough trails.

Socks

Socks serve two purposes: to wick sweat away from skin and to provide cushioning. Cotton socks aren't very good for hiking, except in extremely dry environments, because they retain moisture that can lead to blisters. Wool socks or liner socks work best. You'll want to look for three-season socks, also known as trekking socks. While a little thicker than summer socks, their extra cushioning generally prevents blisters. Also, make sure kids don't put on holey socks; that's just inviting blisters.

Layering

On all but hot, dry days, when hiking you should wear multiple layers of clothing that provide various levels of protection against sweat, heat loss, wind and potentially rain. Layering works because the type of clothing you select for each stratum serves a different function, such as wicking moisture or shielding against wind. In addition, trapped air between each layer of clothing is warmed by your body heat. Layers also can be added or taken off as needed.

Generally, you need three layers. Closest to your skin is the wicking layer, which pulls perspiration away from the body and into the next layer, where it evaporates. Exertion from walking means you will sweat and generate heat, even if the weather is cold. The second layer provides insulation, which helps keep you warm. The last layer is a water-resistant shell that protects you from rain, wind, snow and sleet.

As the seasons and weather change, so does the type of clothing you select for each layer. The first layer ought to be a loose-fitting T-shirt in summer, but in winter and on other cold days you might opt for a long-sleeved moisture-wicking synthetic material, like polypropylene. During winter, the next layer probably also should cover the neck, which often is exposed to the elements. A turtleneck works fine, but preferably not one made of cotton. The third layer in winter, depending on the temperature, could be a wool sweater, a half-zippered long sleeved fleece jacket, or a fleece vest.

You might even add a fourth layer of a hooded parka with pockets, made of material that can block wind and resist water. Gloves or mittens as well as a hat also are necessary on cold days.

Headgear

Half of all body heat is lost through the head, hence the hiker's adage, "If your hands are cold, wear a hat." In cool, wet weather, wearing a hat is at least good for avoiding hypothermia, a potentially deadly condition in which heat loss occurs faster than the body can generate it. Children are more susceptible to hypothermia than adults.

Especially during summer, a hat with a wide brim is useful in keeping the sun out of eyes. It's also nice should rain start falling.

For young children, get a hat with a chin strap. They like to play with their hats, which will fly off in a wind gust if not fastened some way to the child.

Sunglasses

Sunglasses are an absolute must if walking through open areas exposed to the sun and in winter when you can suffer from snow blindness. Look for 100% UV-protective shades, which provide the best screen.

Equipment

A couple of principles should guide your purchases. First,

the longer and more complex the hike, the more equipment you'll need. Secondly, your general goal is to go light. Since you're on a day hike, the amount of gear you'll need is a fraction of what backpackers shown in magazines and catalogues usually carry. Still, the inclination of most day hikers is to not carry enough equipment. For the lightness issue, most gear today is made with titanium and siliconized nylon, ensuring it is sturdy yet fairly light. While the following list of what you need may look long, it won't weigh much.

Backpacks

Sometimes called daypacks (for day hikes or for kids), backpacks are essential to carry all of the essentials you need – snacks, first-aid kit, extra clothing.

For day hiking, you'll want to get an internal frame, in which the frame giving the backpack its shape is inside the pack's fabric so it's not exposed to nature. Such frames usually are lightweight and comfortable. External frames have the frame outside the pack, so they are exposed to the elements. They are excellent for long hikes into the backcountry when you must carry heavy loads.

As kids get older, and especially after they've been hiking for a couple of years, they'll want a "real" backpack. Unfortunately, most backpacks for kids are overbuilt and too heavy. Even light ones that safely can hold up to 50 pounds are inane for most children.

When buying a daypack for your child, look for sternum straps, which help keep the strap on the shoulders. This is vital for prepubescent children, as they do not have the broad shoulders that come with adolescence, meaning packs likely will slip off and onto their arms, making them uncomfortable and difficult to carry. Don't buy a backpack that a child will "grow into." Backpacks that don't fit well simply will lead to sore shoulder and back muscles and could result in poor posture.

Also, consider purchasing a daypack with a hydration system for kids. This will help ensure they drink a lot of water. More on this later when we get to canteens.

Before hitting the trail, always check your children's backpacks to make sure that they have not overloaded them. Kids think they need more than they really do. They also tend to overestimate their own ability to carry stuff. Sibling rivalries often lead to children packing more than they should in their rucksacks, too. Don't let them overpack "to teach them a lesson," though, as it can damage bones and turn the hike into a bad experience.

A good rule of thumb is no more than 25 percent capacity. Most upper elementary school kids can carry only about 10 pounds for any short distance. Subtract the weight of the backpack, and that means only 4-5 pounds in the backpack. Overweight children will need to carry a little less than this or they'll quickly be out of breath.

Child carriers

You'll have to carry infant and toddlers. Until infants can hold their heads up, which usually doesn't happen until about four to six months of age, a front pack (like a Snugli or Baby Bjorn) is best. It keeps the infant close for warmth and balances out your backpack. At the same time, though, you must watch for baby overheating in a front pack, so you'll need to remove the infant from your body at rest stops.

Once children reach about 20 pounds, they typically can hold their heads up and sit on their own. At that point, you'll want a baby carrier (sometimes called a child carrier or baby backpack), which can transfer the infant's weight to your hips when you walk. You'll not only be comfortable, but your child will love it too.

Look for a baby carrier that is sturdy yet lightweight. Your child is going to get heavier as time passes, so about the only way you can counteract this is to reduce the weight of the items you use to carry things. The carrier also should have adjustment points, as you don't want your child to outgrow the carrier too soon. A padded waist belt and padded shoulder straps are necessary for your comfort. The carrier should provide some kind of head and neck support if you're hauling an infant. It also should offer back support for children of all ages, and leg holes should be wide enough so there's no chafing. You want to be able to load your infant without help, so it should be stable enough to stand that way when you take it off the child can sit in it for a moment while you get turned around. Stay away from baby carriers with only shoulder straps, as you need the waist belt to help shift the child's weight to your hips for more comfortable walking.

Fanny packs

Also known as a belt bag, a fanny pack is virtually a must for anyone with a baby carrier, as you can't otherwise lug a backpack. If your significant other is with you, he or she can carry the backpack, of course. Still, the fanny pack also is a good alternative to a backpack in hot weather, as it will reduce back sweat.

If you have only one or two kids on a hike, or if they also are old enough to carry daypacks, your fanny pack need not be large. A mid-size pouch can carry at least 200 cubic inches of supplies, which is more than enough to accommodate all the materials you need. A good fanny pack also has a spot for hooking canteens to.

Canteens

Canteens or plastic bottles filled with water are vital for any hike, no matter how short the trail. You'll need to have enough of them to carry about two pints of water per person for every hour of hiking.

Trekking poles

Also known as walking poles or walking sticks, trekking poles are necessary for maintaining stability on uneven or wet surfaces and to help reduce fatigue. The latter makes them useful on even surfaces. By transferring weight to the arms, a trekking pole can reduce stress on your knees and lower back, allowing you to maintain a better posture and to go farther.

If an adult with a baby or toddler on your back, you'll primarily want a trekking pole to help you maintain your balance, even if on a flat surface, and to help absorb some of the impact of your step.

Graphite tips provide the best traction. A basket just above the tip is a good idea so the stick doesn't sink into mud or sand. Angled cork handles are ergonomic and help absorb sweat from your hands so they don't blister. A strap on the handle to wrap around your hand is useful so the stick doesn't slip out. Telescopic poles are a good idea as you can adjust them as needed based on the terrain you're hiking and as kids grow to accommodate their height.

The pole also needs to be sturdy enough to handle rugged terrain, as you don't want a pole that bends when you press it to the ground. Spring-loaded shock absorbers help when heading down a steep incline but aren't necessary. Indeed, for a short walk across flat terrain, the right length stick is about all you need.

Carabiners

Carabiners are metal loops, vaguely shaped like a D, with a sprung or screwed gate. You'll find that hooking a couple of them to your backpack or fanny pack useful in many ways. For example, if you need to dig through a fanny pack, you can hook the strap of your trekking pole to it. Your hat, camera straps, first-aid kit, and a number of other objects also can connect to them. Hook carabiners to your fanny pack or backpack upon purchasing them so you don't forget them when packing. Small carabiners with sprung gates are inexpensive, but they do have a limited life span of a couple of dozen hikes.

Navigational Tools

Paper maps

Paper maps may sound passé in this age of GPS, but you'll find the variety and breadth of view they offer to be useful. During the planning process, a paper map (even if viewing it online), will be far superior to a GPS device. On the hike, you'll also want a backup to GPS. Or like many casual hikers, you may not own GPS at all, which makes paper maps indispensable.

Standard road maps (which includes printed guides and handmade trail maps) show highways and locations of cities and parks. Maps included in guidebooks, printed guides handed out at parks, and those that are hand-drawn tend to be designed like road maps, and often carry the same positives and negatives.

Topographical maps give contour lines and other important details for crossing a landscape. You'll find them invaluable on a hike into the wilds. The contour lines' shape and their spacing on a topo map show the form and steepness of a hill or bluff, unlike the standard road map and most brochures and hand-drawn trail maps. You'll also know if you're in a woods, which is marked in green, or in a clearing, which is marked in white. If you get lost, figuring out where you are and how to get to where you need to be will be much easier with such information.

Aerial photos offer a view from above that is rendered exactly as it would look from an airplane. Thanks to Google and other online services, you can get fairly detailed pictures of the landscape. Such pictures are an excellent resource when researching a hiking trail. Unfortunately, those pictures don't label what a feature is or what it's called, as would a topo map. Unless there's a stream, determining if a feature is a valley bottom or a ridgeline also can be difficult. Like topo maps, satellite and aerial photos can be out of date a few years.

GPS

By using satellites, the global positioning system can find your spot on the Earth to within 10 feet. With a GPS device, you can preprogram the trailhead location and mark key turns and landmarks as well as the hike's end point. This mobile map is a powerful technological tool that almost certainly ensures you won't get lost – so long as you've correctly programmed the information. GPS also can calculate travel time and act as a compass, a barometer and altimeter, making such devices virtually obsolete on a hike.

In remote areas, however, reception is spotty at best for GPS, rendering your mobile map worthless. A GPS device also runs on batteries, and there's always a chance they will go dead. Or you may drop your device, breaking it in the process. Their screens are small, and sometimes you need a large paper map to get a good sense of the natural landmarks around you.

Compass

Like a paper map, a compass is indispensable even if you use GPS. Should your GPS no longer function, the compass then can be used to tell you which direction you're heading. A protractor compass is best for hiking. Beneath the compass needle is a transparent base with lines to help your orient yourself. The compass often serves as a magnifying glass to help you make out map details. Most protractor compasses also come with a lanyard for easy carrying.

Food and Water

Water

As water is the heaviest item you'll probably carry, there is a temptation to not take as much as one should. Don't skimp on the amount of water you bring, though; after all, it's the one supply your body most needs. It's always better to end up having more water than needed than returning to your vehicle dehydrated.

How much water should you take? Adults need at least a quart for every two hours hiking. Children need to drink about a quart every two hours of walking and more if the weather is hot or dry. To keep kids hydrated, have them drink at every rest stop.

Don't presume there will be drinking water on the hiking trail. Most trails outside of urban areas lack such an amenity. In addition, don't drink water from local streams, lakes, rivers or ponds. There's no way to tell if local water is safe or not. As soon as you have consumed half of your water supply, you should turn around for the vehicle.

Food

Among the many wonderful things about hiking is that

snacking between meals isn't frowned upon. Unless going on an all-day hike in which you'll picnic along the way, you want to keep everyone in your hiking party fed, especially as hunger can lead to lethargic and discontented children. It'll also keep young kids from snacking on the local flora or dirt. Before hitting the trail, you'll want to repackage as much of the food as possible as products sold at grocery stores tend to come in bulky packages that take up space and add a little weight to your backpack. Place the food in re-sealable plastic bags.

Bring a variety of small snacks for rest stops. You don't want kids filling up on snacks, but you do need them to maintain their energy levels if they're walking or to ensure they don't turn fussy if riding in a child carrier. Go for complex carbohydrates and proteins for maintaining energy. Good options include dried fruits, jerky, nuts, peanut butter, prepared energy bars, candy bars with a high protein content (nuts, peanut butter), crackers, raisins and trail mix (called "gorp"). A number of trail mix recipes are available online; you and your children may want to try them out at home to see which ones you collectively like most.

Salty treats rehydrate better than sweet treats do. Chocolate and other sweets are fine if they're not all that's served, but remember they also tend to lead to thirst and to make sticky messes. Whichever snacks you choose, don't experiment with food on the trail. Bring what you know kids will like.

Give the first snack within a half-hour of leaving the trailhead or you risk children becoming tired and whiny from low energy levels. If kids start asking for them every few steps even after having something to eat at the last rest stop, consider timing snacks to reaching a seeable landmark, such as, "We'll get out the trail mix when we reach that bend up ahead."

Milk for infants

If you have an infant or unweaned toddler with you, milk is as necessary as water. Children who only drink breastfed milk but don't have their mother on the hike require that you have breast-pumped milk in an insulated beverage container (such as a Thermos) that can keep it cool to avoid spoiling. Know how much the child drinks and at what frequency so you can bring enough. You'll also need to carry the child's bottle and feeding nipples. Bring enough extra water in your canteen so you can wash out the bottle after each feeding. A handkerchief can be used to dry bottles between feedings.

Don't forget the baby's pacifier. Make sure it has a string and hook attached so it connects to the baby's outfit and isn't lost.

What not to bring

Avoid soda and other caffeinated beverages, alcohol, and energy pills. The caffeine will dehydrate children as well as you. Alcohol has no place on the trail; you need your full faculties when making decisions and driving home. Energy pills essentially are a stimulant and like alcohol can lead to bad calls. If you're tired, get some sleep and hit the trail another day.

First-aid Kit

After water, this is the most essential item you can carry.

A first-aid kit should include:

- Adhesive bandages of various types and sizes, especially butterfly bandages (for younger kids, make sure they're colorful kid bandages)
- Aloe vera
- Anesthetic (such as Benzocaine)
- Antacid (tablets)

- Antibacterial (aka antibiotic) ointment (such as Neosporin or Bacitracin)
- Anti-diarrheal tablets (for adults only, as giving this to a child is controversial)
- Anti-itch cream or calamine lotion
- Antiseptics (such as hydrogen peroxide, iodine or Betadine, Mercuroclear, rubbing alcohol)
- Baking soda
- Breakable (or instant) ice packs
- Cotton swabs
- Disposable syringe (w/o needle)
- Epipen (if children or adults have allergies)
- Fingernail clippers (your multi-purpose tool might have this, and if so you can dispense with it)
- Gauze bandage
- Gauze compress pads (2x2 individually wrapped pad)
- Hand sanitizer (use this in place of soap)
- Liquid antihistamine (not Benadryl tablets, however, as children should take liquid not pills; be aware that liquid antihistamines may cause drowsiness)
- Medical tape
- Moisturizer containing an anti-inflammatory
- Mole skin
- Pain reliever (aka aspirin; for children's pain relief, use liquid acetaminophen such Tylenol or liquid ibuprofen; never give aspirin to a child under 12)
- Poison ivy cream (for treatment)
- Poison ivy soap
- Powdered sports drinks mix or electrolyte additives
- Sling
- Snakebite kit
- Thermometer

- Tweezers (your multi-purpose tool may have this allowing you to dispense with it)
- Water purification tablets

If infants are with you, be sure to also carry teething ointment (such as Orajel) and diaper rash treatment.

Many of the items should be taken out of their store packaging to make placement in your fanny pack or backpack easier. In addition, small amounts of some items – such as baking soda and cotton swabs – can be placed inside re-sealable plastic bags, since you won't need the whole amount purchased.

Make sure the first-aid items are in a waterproof container. A re-sealable plastic zipper bag is perfectly fine. If hiking in a humid or wet climate, be sure to replace the adhesive bandages every couple of months, as they can deteriorate in the moistness. Also, check your first-aid kit every few trips and after any hike in which you've just used it, so that you can replace used components and to make sure medicines haven't expired.

If you have older elementary-age kids and teenagers who've been trained in first aid, giving them a kit to carry as well as yourself is a good idea. Should they find themselves lost or if you cannot get to them for a few moments, the kids might need to provide very basic first aid to one another.

Hiking with Children: Attitude Adjustment

To enjoy hiking with kids, you'll first have to adopt your child's perspective. Simply put, we must learn to hike on our kids' schedules – even though they may not know that's what we're doing.

Compared to adults, kids can't walk as far, they can't walk as fast, and they will grow bored more quickly. Every step we take requires three for them. In addition, early walkers, up to two years of age, prefer to wander than to "hike." Preschool kids will start to walk the trail, but at a rate of only about a mile per hour. With stops, that can turn a three-mile hike into a four-hour journey. Kids also won't be able to hike as steep of trails as you or handle as inclement of weather as you might.

This all may sound limiting, especially to long-time backpackers used to racking up miles or bagging peaks on their hikes, but it's really not. While you may have to put off some backcountry and mountain climbing trips for a while, it also opens to you a number of great short trails and nature hikes with spectacular sights that you may have otherwise skipped because they weren't challenging enough.

So sure, you'll have to make some compromises, but the payout is high. You're not personally on the hike to get a workout but to spend quality time with your children.

Family Dog

Dogs are part of the family, and if you have children, they'll want to share the hiking experience with their pets. In turn, dogs will have a blast on the trail, some larger dogs can be used as Sherpas, and others will defend against threatening animals.

But there is a downside to dogs. Many will chase animals and so run the risk of getting lost or injured. Also, a doggy bag will have to be carried for dog pooh – yeah, it's natural, but also inconsiderate to leave for other hikers to smell and for their kids to step in. In addition, most dogs almost always will lose a battle against a threatening animal, so there's a price to be paid for your safety.

Many places where you'll hike solve the dilemma for you as dogs aren't allowed on their trails. Dogs are verboten on some state and national parks trails but usually permitted on those in national forests. Always check with the park ranger before heading to the trail.

If you can bring a dog, make sure it is well behaved and friendly to others. You don't need your dog biting another hiker while unnecessarily defending the family.

Rules of the Trail

Ah, the woods or a wide open meadow, peaceful and quiet, not a single soul around for miles. Now you and your children can do whatever you want.

Not so fast.

Act like wild animals on a hike, and you'll destroy the very aspects of the wilds that make them so attractive. You're also likely to end up back in civilization, specifically an emergency room. And there are other people around. Just as you would wish them to treat you courteously, so you and your children should do the same for them.

Let's cover how to act civilized on the trail.

Minimize damage to your surroundings

When on the trail, follow the maxim of "Leave no trace." Obviously, you shouldn't toss litter on the ground, start rockslides, or pollute water supplies. How much is damage and how much is good-natured exploring is a gray area, of course. Most serious backpackers will say you should never pick up objects, break branches, throw rocks, pick flowers, and so on – the idea is not to disturb the environment at all.

Good luck getting a four-year-old to think like that. The good news is a four-year-old won't be able to throw around many rocks or break most branches.

Still, children from their first hike into the wilderness should be taught to respect nature and to not destroy their environment. While you might overlook a preschooler hurling rocks into a puddle, they can be taught to sniff rather than pick flowers. As they grow older, you can teach them the value of leaving the rock alone. Regardless of age, don't allow children to write on boulders or carve into trees.

Many hikers split over picking berries. To strictly abide by the "minimize damage" principle, you wouldn't pick any berries at all. Kids, however, are likely to find great pleasure in eating blackberries, currants and thimbleberries as ambling down the trail. Personally, I don't see any problem enjoying a few berries if the long-term payoff is a respect and love for nature. To minimize damage, teach them to only pick berries they can reach from the trail so they don't trample plants or deplete food supplies for animals. They also should only pick what they'll eat.

Collecting is another issue. In national and most state and county parks, taking rocks, flower blossoms and even pine cones is illegal. Picking flowers moves many species, especially if they are rare and native, one step closer to extinction. Archeological ruins are extremely fragile, and even touching them can damage a site.

But on many trails, especially gem trails, collecting is part of the adventure. Use common sense – if the point of the trail is to find materials to collect, such as a gem trail, take judiciously, meaning don't overcollect. Otherwise, leave it there.

Sometimes the trail crosses private land. If so, walking around fields, not through them, always is best or you could damage a farmer's crops.

Pack out what you pack in

Set the example as a parent: Don't litter yourself; whenever stopping, pick up whatever you've dropped; and always require kids to pick up after themselves when they litter. In the spirit of "Leave no trace," try to leave the trail cleaner than you found it, so if you come across litter that's safe to pick up, do so and bring it back to a trash bin in civilization. Given this, you may want to bring a plastic bag to carry out garbage.

Picking up litter doesn't just mean gum and candy wrappers but also some organic materials that take a long time to decompose and aren't likely to be part of the natural environment you're hiking. In particular, these include peanut shells, orange peelings, and eggshells.

Burying litter, by the way, isn't viable. Either animals or erosion soon will dig it up, leaving it scattered around the trail and woods.

Stay on the trail

Hiking off trail means potentially damaging fragile growth. Following this rule not only ensures you minimize damage but is also a matter of safety. Off trail is where kids most likely will encounter dangerous animals and poisonous plants. Not being able to see where they're stepping also increases the likelihood of falling and injuring themselves. Leaving the trail raises the chances of getting lost. Staying on the trail also means staying out of caves, mines or abandoned structures you may encounter. They are usually dangerous places.

Finally, never let children take a shortcut on a switchback trail. Besides putting them on steep ground upon which they could slip, their impatient act causes the switchback to erode.

Trail Dangers

On Minnesota trails, two common dangers face hikers: ticks and poison ivy/sumac. Both can make miserable your time on the trail or once back home. Fortunately, both threats are easily avoidable and treatable.

Ticks

One of the greatest dangers comes from the smallest of creatures: ticks. Both the wood and the deer tick are common in Minnesota and can infect people with Lyme disease.

Ticks usually leap onto people from the top of a grass blade as you brush against it, so walking in the middle of the trail away from high plants is a good idea. Wearing a hat, a long sleeve shirt tucked into pants, and pants tucked into shoes or socks, also will keep ticks off you, though this is not foolproof as they sometimes can hook onto clothing. A tightly woven cloth provides the best protection, however. Children can pick up a tick that has hitchhiked onto the family dog, so outfit Rover and Queenie with a tick-repelling collar.

After hiking into an area where ticks live, you'll want to examine your children's bodies (as well as your own) for them. Check warm, moist areas of the skin, such as under the arms, the groin and head hair. Wearing light-colored clothing helps make the tiny tick easier to spot.

To get rid of a tick that has bitten your child, drip either disinfectant or rubbing alcohol on the bug, so it will loosen its grip. Grip the tick close to its head, slowly pulling it away from the skin. This hopefully will prevent it from releasing saliva that spreads disease. Rather than kill the tick, keep it in a plastic bag so that medical professionals can analyze it should disease symptoms appear. Next, wash the bite area with soap and water then apply antiseptic.

In the days after leaving the woods, also check for signs of disease from ticks. Look for bulls-eye rings, a sign of Lyme disease. Other symptoms include a large red rash, joint pain, and flu-like symptoms. Indications of Rocky Mountain spotted fever include headache, fever, severe muscle aches, and a spotty rash first on palms and feet soles that spread, all beginning about two days after the bite.

If any of these symptoms appear, seek medical attention immediately. Fortunately, antibiotics exist to cure most tick-related diseases.

Poison ivy/sumac

Often the greatest danger in the wilds isn't our own clumsiness or foolhardiness but various plants we encounter. The good news is that we mostly have to force the encounter with flora. Touching the leaves of either poison ivy or poison sumac in particular results in an itchy, painful rash. Each plant's sticky resin, which causes the reaction, clings to clothing and hair, so you may not have "touched" a leaf, but once your hand runs against the resin on shirt or jeans, you'll probably get the rash.

To avoid touching these plants, you'll need to be able to identify each one. Remember the "Leaves of three, let it be" rule for poison ivy. Besides groups of three leaflets, poison ivy has shiny green leaves that are red in spring and fall. Poison sumac's leaves are not toothed as are non-poisonous sumac, and in autumn their leaves turn scarlet. Be forewarned that even after leaves fall off, poison oak's stems can carry some of the itchy resin.

By staying on the trail and walking down its middle rather than the edges, you are unlikely to come into contact with this pair of irritating plants. That probably is the best preventative. Poison ivy barrier creams also can be helpful, but they only temporarily block the resin. This lulls you into a false sense of safety, and so you may not bother to watch for poison ivy.

To treat poison ivy/sumac, wash the part of the body that has touched the plant with poison ivy soap and cold water.

Poison ivy might look pretty, but it still will cause a rash if touched. Always remember the hiker's maxim: "Leaves of three, let it be."

This will erode the oily resin, so it'll be easier to rinse off. If you don't have any of this special soap, plain soap sometimes will work if used within a half-hour of touching the plant. Apply a poison ivy cream and get medical attention immediately. Wearing gloves, remove any clothing (including shoes) that has touched the plants, washing them and the worn gloves right away.

For more about these topics and many others, pick up this author's **Hikes with Tykes: A Practical Guide to Day Hiking with Kids**. You also can find tips online at the author's **DayHikingTrails** blog (*hikeswithtykes.blogspot.com*). We'll see ya' on the trail!

About the Author

Rob Bignell is a long-time hiker, editor, and author of the popular "Hikes with Tykes," "Headin' to the Cabin," "Hittin' the Trail," and "Best Sights to See" guidebooks and several other titles. He and his son Kieran have been hiking together for more than a decade. Rob has served as an infantryman in the Army National Guard and taught middle school students in New Mexico and Wisconsin. His newspaper work has won several national and state journalism awards, from editorial writing to sports reporting. In 2001, *The Prescott Journal*, which he served as managing editor of, was named Wisconsin's Weekly Newspaper of the Year. Rob and Kieran live in Wisconsin.

CHECK OUT ALL THESE GREAT HIKING BOOKS BY THE AUTHOR

"Best Sights to See" series:

- America's National Parks
- Great Smoky Mountain National Park
- Indiana Dunes National Park
- Joshua Tree National Park
- Rocky Mountain National Park
- Voyageurs National Park
- White Sands National Park

"Hikes with Tykes" series:

- Hikes with Tykes: A Practical Guide to Day Hiking with Children
- Hikes with Tykes: Games and Activities

"Headin' to the Cabin" series:

- Day Hiking Trails of Northeast Minnesota
- Day Hiking Trails of Northwest Wisconsin

"Hittin' the Trail" series:

California

- Palm Springs and the Coachella Valley

Minnesota

- Best Minnesota Autumn Hikes
- Best Minnesota Wildflower Hikes
- Gooseberry Falls State Park
- Split Rock Lighthouse State Park

Minnesota/Wisconsin

- Interstate State Park

- St. Croix National Scenic Riverway

Wisconsin

- Barron County
- Bayfield County
- Best Wisconsin Autumn Hikes
- Best Wisconsin Wildflower Hikes
- Burnett County (ebook only)
- Chippewa Valley (Eau Claire, Chippewa, Dunn, Pepin counties)
- Crex Meadows Wildlife Area (ebook only)
- Douglas County
- Polk County
- St. Croix County
- Sawyer County
- Washburn County

National parks

- Grand Canyon National Park (ebook only)

GET CONNECTED!

Follow the author to learn about other great trails and for useful hiking tips:

- Blog: *hikeswithtykes.blogspot.com*
- Facebook: *dld.bz/fBq2C*
- Pinterest: *pinterest.com/rbignell41*
- Twitter: *twitter.com/dayhikingtrails*
- Website: *dayhikingtrails.wordpress.com*

If you enjoyed this book,
please take a few moments to write a review of it.
www.amazon.com/dp/B09CKK6H3H
Thank you!